Voices, Places

DAVID MASON

VOICES, PLACES

ESSAYS

PAUL DRY BOOKS
Philadelphia 2018

First Paul Dry Books Edition, 2018

Paul Dry Books, Inc.
Philadelphia, Pennsylvania
www.pauldrybooks.com

Printed in the United States of America

For Chrissy

Contents

EXILES, ECCENTRICS, IMMIGRANTS

VOICES, PLACES

Preface: Reading in Place

> If you have a strong first world and a strong set of relationships then in some part of you you are always free, you can walk the world because you know where you belong, you have some place to come back to.
>
> —Seamus Heaney

> If you don't know where you are, you don't know who you are.
>
> —Wendell Berry, as paraphrased by
> Wallace Stegner

One can be a reader or a writer anywhere. I grew up in Washington State, suffering the delusion that literature must exist in some distant, glamorous locale, so I traveled. What I learned was that place mattered, voice mattered, but no one can tell us where or how these things are to be found. My "first world," in Seamus Heaney's phrase, had a glamour of its own, a weather of its own, even a budding literature of its own. It stayed with me when I went elsewhere.

In 1974 I went to sea, looking for experience. One extended anchorage, Dutch Harbor, Alaska, was a ghost town of weathered barracks and Quonset huts left over from World War

II. It was a small island, Amaknak, in the bay of a larger one, Unalaska, in a barebacked archipelago between the North Pacific and the Bering Sea. Some would call it precisely the middle of nowhere—one of the writers considered in this book, the poet Thomas McGrath, was stationed there in the war and would have seen much of what I saw. A Russian Orthodox church stood with its onion dome in the one scarcely populated village. A volcano with a Russian name rose in winter like a white pyramid. The place was desolately beautiful, and to a boy who turned twenty working on ships and fishing boats in those islands, it was haunted. Japanese planes had bombed Dutch Harbor not long after the attack on Hawaii, so to stand among the windswept hills and ruins was to feel the devastating swirl of empires—Russia, Japan, the United States—and the shy ongoingness of displaced Aleuts. History was not an abstraction, humanity was not an idea, even in this No Man's Land, this berated wildness of rusty wire and crumbling bunkers.

Events happened. Nixon resigned, and the following spring (I was in Scotland by then) Saigon fell. Events were like pebbles dropping in the dark salt water of the bay.

I kept a journal in Alaska full of youthful ruminations: "My place is to be out of place, and to write about it." The barracks haunted me. Men had lived in them, preparing for the landing to recapture Attu from the Japanese. "All this and Attu," they joked. My father's war—it lingered in the weather and in my blood. A place with no statues, no monuments, no museums, one bar, one church, one school, one mercantile store—the place was a readable vacancy, like walking through a dream.

I had not seen much of the world, but with money made in Alaska I would set out in 1975 to hitchhike the perimeter of the British Isles, with brief forays to France, Spain, and Ireland. I would be a traveler, accumulating stamps and visas in my passport from all over the world. I would live in Greece, travel to Turkey, India, Mexico, and the Antipodes, but my experience was always that of a reader, a body in time. All places are stories, all stories places. If they are alert, the itinerant and the stay-at-home might have nearly the same experience of reading and being.

As a young reader steeping himself in Melville and Tolstoy, Chekhov and Dostoyevsky, Homer and Seferis, I sensed that reading, too, was a form of travel. Reading was time, duration, and if it was any good it changed and moved you. It relocated you, even disoriented you like the protagonist in a game of Blind Man's Bluff. Reading was another way of being alive in the world, born and reborn in books, and it made you understand that the world was more than one thing. A lifetime of travel and a lifetime of reading have been related. Every new encounter has also been a renewed encounter with my first world and the curiosity it inspired.

WHEN I SHOWED HER the title article of this book, my wife congratulated me on writing an essay without a point. "Voices, Places" arose from experiences I could not really connect—Greece, Venice, Idaho—and yet I had been there. They were connected in my own body-memory. My essay became lyric, fragmented, made up of associations as much as ideas, deliberately avoiding the yoke of a thesis. Assembling this book has also been a matter of associations. I chose pieces that dealt specifically with travel, with ruminations on eccentricity, exile and expatriation, and with places as far-flung as the American West, Australia, Asia, and Greece. Many of these pieces began as book reviews or commissioned works, so they weren't written with the idea that they belonged together between covers. I had to decide whether to include them by a process of association and elimination, leaving a little room for the unstated and the whimsical.

Essays in the first section are often located in Greece, but most often as it is experienced by foreigners, a heritage of reinvented culture and personality. In Greece I met two great travelers, Patrick Leigh Fermor and Bruce Chatwin, who taught by example what it meant to cherish locale, even while estranged from it. My little stone hut next to Paddy's villa in a bay south of Kardamyli gave me proximity to all the writer pilgrims who passed through. It was the most intoxicating period of reading I have ever known, and I have as a result always associated literature with footloose and unencumbered living. Paddy and Joan Leigh Fermor lent me books, which I read in the shade of a cypress tree or next to a banana grove on land they had once hoped to own. I just missed getting to know Kevin Andrews, but his evocations of Greek life have been no less important to me. The other thread connecting essays in the opening section is the postcolonial world—Tasmania, English and Australian eccentricity, and the reaches of empire described by Edward FitzGerald and Pankaj Mishra.

Pieces in my second section consider exiles and expatriates like Conrad, Pound, Joyce, and Auden, but also some writers who will be less familiar to most readers. Kevin Hart was born in England and now teaches in Virginia, yet is best known as an Australian poet. Les Murray, briefly considered here, is paired with another Australian I happen to love, Cally Conan-Davies. An indulgence on my part allows for associations no one else could possibly make.

Finally, the third section of the book arrives closer to my first world. The title essay is followed by pieces on writers of the American West, from the California of Jeffers to the Rocky Mountains of Belle Turnbull. Each of the figures considered in this grouping can be called an eccentric in terms of the canon of American literature, however we define it. Eccentricity, as the word implies, is a form of displacement, standing outside the circle of inclusion, and I have always found it an attractive quality in a writer.

Editors who first published these pieces, sometimes in different form, provided helpful suggestions along the way. These include Robert Messenger at *The Wall Street Journal*, George

Core and Leigh Anne Couch at *The Sewanee Review,* and Paula Deitz and Ron Koury at *The Hudson Review.* I also thank the editors of *Antipodes, Think Journal,* and *Voltage Poetry.* The biographical essay on Thomas McGrath was commissioned by Jay Parini for a Scribner's *American Writers* volume, and "Belle Turnbull's Western Narrative" was commissioned by David J. Rothman for a book introducing her work to new readers. I include Paul Dry and his staff at Paul Dry Books in my hearty thanks.

Travelers

Letter from Tasmania

You find yourself thinking *England.* Then you think *No, Wales. No, Scotland.* But despite a very British culture, Tasmania is none of these. Nor is it the Pacific Northwest, though its vast tracts of rainforest and giant ferns remind me of home. Tasmania is wonderfully other.

You know you're not in the northern hemisphere when looking at the night sky, locating the Southern Cross and the Magellanic Clouds. And you know when you see the gum trees turning red with new growth in spring instead of red with death in the fall. The world's turned upside down.

A eucalypt forest is far more multifarious than I realized. Diverse types of gum trees appear to mimic deciduous foliage from all over the earth. Then in another glance they are visibly *not* European, *not* North American, *not* of the Indian subcontinent, but a forest you can see into, the trees tattered and shedding—perfect fuel for regular bushfires. And it smells better than any perfume I have ever known. If I could bottle the smell of a eucalypt forest in spring I'd be richer than Ralph Lauren.

Nearly forty-five percent of Tasmania is set aside as parkland, much of it World Heritage. Some of the world's tallest eucalyptus trees grow there. Saving the Tasmanian wilderness from exploitation and development was a milestone in the environmental movement, foundational for Australia's Green Party. The current conservative government, however, seems dead-set on rolling back those gains.

Reading about these developments, Americans must adjust their vocabulary. Here the conservatives are the Liberal Party, while the liberals are Labour. Here Liberals might say with our Republicans, "Drill, baby, drill." Tasmania's economy is the weakest in the country, but to lose its old-growth forests would create a crisis of another kind—an identity crisis. Just what is Tasmania? The license plates say, "Your Natural State." Lose the nature and what have you got?

You've got a lot, it turns out. A city on the rise in Hobart, some fine smaller cities and great cultural institutions—yet it all seems *Tasmanian* because you are never far from the wild, the constant variation of peak and valley, the bush like wave on pale-green wave of life.

We arrived on this heart-shaped island by ferry, *The Spirit of Tasmania*, in December—summer Down Under. Already we had camped in our van for two weeks, traveling through southeastern Australia, and had experienced rising heat. In Victoria's Grampians National Park the heat excited cicadas till their vibrations were literally deafening and we wore ear plugs to hear ourselves think. Yet during our first night in Tassie, as the state is affectionately known, we were snow-drenched in Cradle Mountain National Park—a place that definitely made me think *Scotland*, except for the wombats like miniature bears grazing in the alpine meadows and echidnas sniffing ants from rotten logs in the bush.

The island has been cared for. People clearly take pride in the land, yet its history has been violent. Tasmania's Aborigines were wiped out by disease and massacre. The last full-blood Tasmanian Aborigine, a woman named Truganini, died in 1876. (Some argue that the last person of full blood was Fanny

Cochrane Smith, who lived into the twentieth century.) Now mixed-blood Aborigines claim the heritage—including land rights and social benefits.

Tasmania is both familiar and estranging, cozy and mildly dangerous—all snakes in Tassie can kill you. The land feels deliciously passed over by modern abrasiveness, quite suitable for Hobbits and recluses. My wife was born here, in Hobart, the daughter of an English colonial mother and a father descended from a transported convict. Isolation from the rest of the world once made Tasmania an ideal prison, but the same isolation now seems idyllic.

As we drove the small, winding roads, one startlingly beautiful view of mountains and paddocks full of sheep or cattle following another, I began to call it "the land that time forgot."

EARLY EUROPEAN EXPLORATION of Australia was a comedy of errors. Everyone assumed a *Terra Australis Incognita* lay down there somewhere, but globe-circumnavigating vessels kept missing it. Landings on the continent took place as early as the sixteenth century, but none of them resulted in colonies. Tasmania was officially "discovered" first. Abel Tasman found it in 1642 and called it Van Diemen's Land in honor of his employer, a governor of the Dutch East Indies. The English landed in the 1770s and were more assiduous than other Europeans in their colonization of the continent. Robert Hughes' superb history, *The Fatal Shore* (1987), tells how Australia was first used as a series of work camps for transported criminals. Between 1803 and 1853 some 75,000 convicts were transported to Tasmania alone. One early prison at Macquarie Harbour on the west coast was guarded by headlands and riptides difficult to pass, and surrounded by a wilderness in which escaping convicts starved or were reduced to cannibalism before being captured, flogged, and resentenced.

When you consider that some transported criminals were petty thieves, others political dissidents from Ireland, you can see the injustice of the penal system even more clearly. Ships carrying prisoners to this unknown land were often recommissioned slavers, so overcrowded and unsanitary that typhus killed many on board.

Perhaps Dickens' Magwitch came to Tasmania. Remember the Hulks near the mouth of the Thames where Pip first encountered his convict:

> By the light of the torches, we saw the black Hulk lying out a little way from the mud of the shore, like a wicked Noah's ark. Cribbed and barred and moored by massive rusty chains, the prison-ship seemed in my young eyes to be ironed like the prisoners.

In *Great Expectations* the policy of transportation is not merely a plot device, but creates a form of social equality the young snobbish Pip needs to learn. Another novel, Marcus Clarke's Tasmanian classic, *For the Term of His Natural Life*, is often melodramatic, Gothic in sensibility, but notable for vivid descriptive passages and impressive reportage, like this about the "classless society" of a convict ship:

> Old men, young men, and boys, stalwart burglars and highway robbers, slept side by side with wizened pickpockets or cunning-featured area-sneaks. The forger occupied the same berth with the body-snatcher. The man of education learned strange secrets of housebreakers' craft, and the vulgar ruffian of St. Giles took lessons of self-control from the keener intellect of the professional swindler.

Australia's convict past contributed to the social leveling you still feel among its people today, a lack of reverence for money or station or power, anarchic humor and the culture of mateship. Australians don't make a lot of idealistic noise and would never call themselves, as Americans are wont to do, "the greatest nation on earth."

Marcus Clarke was remarkable. Born and educated in London, he emigrated to Australia and tried to learn farming in Victoria, but was soon writing stories instead of tilling the soil. A brief visit to Tasmania in 1870 inspired him to write his most famous book, which was serialized in the *Australasian Journal* over the following two years. Clarke wrote a lot, but money troubles followed him and are said to have helped cause his death at only thirty-five.

Halfway through our month in Tasmania, we visited one of his novel's settings, Port Arthur, the most famous prison on the island and now a World Heritage site on a serene harbor tucked into the western flank of Carnarvon Bay, roughly one hundred kilometers southeast of Hobart. The Commandant's spacious house and gardens look out on Mason's Cove, where longboats would have moored, and nearby are several large prison complexes, a hospital, an asylum, a huge Victorian garden, and a well-appointed church. Port Arthur looks like a ruined English village rather than the setting of hard labor and floggings. The brick buildings reflect evolving theories of incarceration. Should men live under constant watch as in Jeremy Bentham's Panoptic Prison, or should they be left in solitary confinement—Benjamin Rush's theory—to take stock of their sins and repair themselves? What is a person? Novelists and jailers ask the same question.

Escape from Port Arthur was impossible. As Clarke puts it,

> The Peninsula of Port Arthur was admirably guarded, signal stations drew a chain round the prison, an armed boat's crew watched each bay, and across the narrow isthmus which connected it with the mainland was a cordon of watch-dogs, in addition to the soldier guard.

That "Dog-Line" at Eaglehawk Neck was a gruesome barrier, with a dozen poorly-fed Cerberuses snapping at anyone trying to get past.

Across from Mason's Cove lies Point Puer, a boys' prison, and just off that a tiny Isle of the Dead. The latter proved well worth a boat trip into the harbor for the tour. Convicts carved the headstones for people of all classes buried there; the misspellings and chiseled corrections are hilarious. A deceased school inspector was "Sincerily regretted by all who knew him." Another fellow was remembered as a "Businessman, Forger, Convict and Author." On a tour of the Isle, the novelist Anthony Trollope asked the Irish gravedigger in residence why he did not keep a vegetable garden. The wizened convict pointed to the ground, reminding Trollope what was already planted on every square inch of land.

Port Arthur is also the site of Australia's worst mass murder. On April 28, 1996, a young man named Martin Bryant drove to the park with a bag of guns and started shooting. He killed methodically all of that day and into the night and the next morning before being captured. Among those he shot point-blank, after first shooting their mother, were two little girls, Alannah and Madeline Mikac. At the end of the massacre thirty-five people lay dead, twenty-three wounded. He chose Port Arthur for the same reason it had made a secure prison—his victims would have no way of escaping.

We had talked about this at a dinner in Hobart, where a new friend of ours recalled hearing, "There's a surfie down in Port Arthur with a gun." Common associations of surfer culture with something illicit come to mind, yet all the surfers I have known are people of quiet integrity. Like fishermen, they have sea-knowledge and look out for each other and help the young learn their skills. Martin Bryant was no "surfie."

The cafe where he did much of his killing has been turned into a memorial and a meditative space in the park. On three of the four sides of a fountain you can read these words:

MAY WE WHO COME TO THIS GARDEN CHERISH LIFE
FOR THE SAKE OF THOSE WHO DIED

CHERISH COMPASSION FOR THE SAKE OF THOSE WHO GAVE AID

CHERISH PEACE FOR THE SAKE OF THOSE IN PAIN

In America massacres nearly as bad as Port Arthur are now regular occurrences and our gun laws hardly change. But Australia is a different sort of society. As my wife puts it, "There's no freedom at the cost of other people." America says, "Don't tread on me and don't mess with my rights." Australia says, "Yes, but look out for your mate at the same time." It's an ethic partly born of the country's convict past.

The Port Arthur Massacre caused immediate national soul-searching, after which Australia enacted some of the toughest gun-control laws in the industrialized world. A nation that began as a prison has produced one of the most stable, law-abiding societies on earth.

MARTIN BRYANT CAME FROM New Town, a neighborhood of Hobart where some of our family live and where my wife's childhood school was located. She and her sister would take the city bus in from Berriedale, their suburb further north, to face the strict discipline and love of the nuns. We arrived in Hobart during the Christmas holiday, just before the summer exodus of January in which many Australian families hit the road and pack the nation's campgrounds. My wife had not been back in her birthplace for three decades, and she wanted me to see how beautiful it was.

Walking through New Town, we saw the hospital where she was born as well as her school with its Eucharistic motto: *Sursum corda* ("Lift up your hearts"). The school was closed, but on the office door we read another motto of a sort common in Australia yet nonexistent in the United States: "As you take your next step remember the first people who walked this land."

Hobart is my idea of the Goldilocks city—"Just right." With a population of more than two hundred thousand, it is large enough for good food and other cultural amenities, complex enough for the usual social problems and dramas, but small enough to be crossed on a bike. Hobart lines the Derwent River—really a large estuary snaking out to Storm Bay and the open sea. On the west side of the Derwent you have Mount Wellington, first noted by William Bligh on one of his voyages. To the east lies Mount Direction like a beacon of the future.

From her bedroom in Berriedale, my wife as a little girl used to look out on a peninsula jutting into the Derwent. It was a magic and forbidden place for her, with an Italian villa and vineyard. Children used to catch pollywogs just below its bluff, but they never tresspassed. Now the grapevines remain but the villa is gone, and in its place the world's strangest art museum has been built.

MONA—the Museum of Old and New Art—is the brainchild of Hobart's most controversial citizen, David Walsh. As it happens, he is exactly my wife's age and also grew up Catholic in a troubled Hobart family. In his youth Walsh rejected the Church and cultivated two different tastes of his own, for art and mathematics. His taste in art is anti-academic, to say the least. He despises the hushed reverence with which most museums treat their treasures and wants art to be a more open playground.

His skill with mathematics made MONA possible. According to "Tasmanian Devil," a profile of Walsh by Tassie novelist Richard Flanagan (*New Yorker*, January 21, 2013), Walsh is a leading member of a gambling syndicate called the Bank Roll. Walsh's algorithms have allowed the syndicate to win huge fortunes at casinos and betting operations around the world.

Walsh built MONA mostly with his own money, and the museum is his Wonderland as much as the people's. He lives in a rooftop apartment with various windows to the underworld he has built, rather like the Wizard of Oz behind his curtain. You can see the extremity of my allusions: Lewis Carroll, Hades, and L. Frank Baum rolled into one. On the day we were there Walsh could be seen out on the grounds, engaged in conversation with museum-goers. Tasmanians enter for free. The rest of us pay admission, but MONA still needs millions to stay afloat. Nobody knows what its future will be.

For the present moment, however, MONA is marvelous. The exhibit we saw was titled "The Red Queen" after Lewis Carroll, and indeed, entering the building is like going down the rabbit hole. Instead of a monument to imperial taste rising from manicured grounds, MONA asks you to descend deep into the peninsula, either by spiral staircase or elevator, following giant walls of rock into Hadean depths. There you find art by painters like Australia's Sidney Nolan in proximity with stranger things—a mummified possum whose open abdomen emits a flurry of insects, an "affectionate couch" named Zizi who makes sweet gurgling sounds when you lie on her, two giant Buddhas—one made of metal, the other of incense ashes—facing each other in a dimly-lit space. There's a wall of water spelling words from news headlines that fall and disappear (as news headlines are apt to do), another wall of projected language and numbers defying comprehension. Both walls invite children and grown-ups to stand in front of them and pose or perform, becoming part of the art, part of the challenge of finding meaning in a data-saturated world.

As a museum devoted to sex and death, MONA has its share of controversial exhibits. One of the basement toilets, for example, is a satirical masterpiece. An unsuspecting patron enters the toilet and takes the accustomed seat, noticing a small pair of binoculars on the counter. Nothing to read, so he naturally looks through the binoculars, and soon notices something, an illuminated object across the room. Very quickly he realizes the object he is staring at is nothing other than a human bum. Soon after, he realizes just whose bum it is, conveyed back to him by a system of mirrors and lights.

"Poets should go and sit in the third toilet on the right," a friend later said in another context. "Most of them are only looking up their own arseholes." I couldn't agree more.

MONA's partially-lit spaces expose the observer-participant to both life and art. The open rooms and pools of illumination allow you to see multiple exhibits at once, sometimes reflecting each other or the people viewing them. There's no respectful distance between art and its viewer. Nothing is labeled. You hold a small iPad as you walk, accessing information only when you want to know more about the works you are seeing. Some of the exhibits are intensely moving. In a room full of old TVs, each one showing a film in which a person from a Turkish village relates his or her life story, you find yourself equally moved by the faces of museum-goers in old armchairs watching these films, or nodding off in front of them.

I was both taken and taken in by the life of the imagination, feeling an unexpectedly sacred energy in the vital irreverence of art. MONA is the only museum I have ever visited that did not at some point fatigue me. The land that time forgot has none of the smugness of cultural capitals, but plenty to teach the world.

WHAT WAS MY FAVORITE DAY in Hobart? The day we rode bikes to MONA and had a coffee on the grounds while chooks wandered among customers gazing across the Derwent from beanbag chairs? Or the day we rode down to Salamanca Place at the harbor and wandered the Taste of Tassie Festival and the old city? On that day the winning boat in the Sydney to Hobart race sailed in.

My wife had known Bob Thomas, one of the world's legendary skippers. In the 1998 race when six sailors died and five yachts sank in a harrowing storm, Thomas lost his instruments but got his boat safely to Hobart using dead reckoning—a feat few others could perform. This year the winning boat was *Wild Oats*, owned by businessman Bob Oatley. We saw it finish just before sunset—its big grey sails and red 7 visible for miles against the hills of Hobart. The mainsail was reefed because they had hit a gale in Storm Bay. I told you—in Tassie you are never far from the wild.

For ten days over Christmas we camped on South Bruny Island, visible from Hobart but a world apart. We stayed in Adventure Bay, a place so little populated we could still imagine the masts and rigging of Cook's and Bligh's ships anchoring there in the eighteenth century. We took a boat trip into the Tasman Sea, then further to the Southern Ocean, where we saw dolphins, seals, and albatrosses. We hiked to the Fluted Cape with its wild orchids and she-oaks and kookaburras. On our way back to camp we found ourselves diverted into an abandoned campground at the foot of the hill. Its buildings— office and toilet blocks—were all intact, though spookily overgrown, and its orchard and paddock were full of wallabies, including two with white fur and pink intelligent eyes. These are the rare painted wallabies of South Bruny. They were like spirit animals, tolerating our presence for a long time before disappearing into the last red light and tall grass where we could not follow them.

Our final campsite on Tassie was far to the northeast, the Bay of Fires, so named because early sailors could see the lights of Aboriginal campfires along the coast. The coast is sacred ground, and I can see why. The beach is bleached white like soft salt crystals. You walk barefoot on the granite headlands at each point and feel the primordial sleeping animal of the earth under your soles. Sometimes Australia seems the beginning of the world.

I'm telling you, Tassie is difficult to describe, though excellent writers have lived here, including the late Christopher Koch, best known for *The Year of Living Dangerously* (1978), and the poet James McAuley, one of the geniuses behind the Ern

Malley Hoax of 1943. The fine philosophical poet Gwen Harwood, who lived much of her life in Hobart, once wrote,

> Language is not a perfect game,
> and if it were, how could we play?
> The world's more than the sum of things
> like moon, sky, centre, body, bed,
> as all the singing masters know.

She's channeling Wittgenstein. Me? I'm trying to channel Tasmania.

Travelers

HERODOTUS AND
PATRICK LEIGH FERMOR

HERODOTUS (484–420 BCE): father of history, teller of lies. A raconteur preserved in prose. A companionable wanderer finding the strange in the familiar and the familiar in the strange. History is a story, after all, and so is travel. When we reduce travel writing to a secondary genre, it is because travel writers too often forget their literary origins in figures like Herodotus, who came at the world with gusto, curiosity, and a knack for the juicy tale. We read *The Histories* for information about the wars between Persia and the Greeks, but the book is so much more than a record of facts. It illuminates the Hellenic world before Alexander tried to unify it in empire, and it treats other civilizations with sympathy, veering sometimes into the fanciful and mythological. "Foreign manners awake his interest," wrote one translator, Aubrey de Sélincourt, "never his antagonism."

The Way of Herodotus, a 2010 book by Justin Marozzi, argues that the ancient historian was the father not only of history but also of the best travel writing—ancestor of modern figures like Robert Byron, Freya Stark, Patrick Leigh Fermor, Jan Morris, and Bruce Chatwin, to name just a few. We don't read these writers for tips on hotels and restaurants, but for literary experience, for enlargement of soul, and for pleasure. Marozzi, who has worked as a journalist and historian, is not as marvelous a writer as those listed above. His lucid prose offers few sentences that would make a reader salivate or shake himself out of a poetic trance. But his enthusiastic book amply demonstrates the contemporary relevance of its subject. Following Herodotus becomes an excuse, as if one were needed, for travel in Turkey, Iraq, Egypt, and Greece. "Outside the world of academe," he announces, "storytelling is prized again, literary talent is admired and thrilling historical narratives are eagerly consumed by record numbers. . . . We have come a long way but have also come full circle. Historians may not realize it, but Herodotus is back."

Having found a vehicle to carry his book, Marozzi sometimes yokes unwieldy baggage to it. Visiting in modern times places Herodotus might or might not have visited in order to write *The Histories* involves much speculation, but it also gives his book the spirit of a quest. Evidence in the search for Herodotus nowhere proves more disappointing than in his birthplace, Bodrum (ancient Halicarnassus), a tourist mecca on the Turkish coast. Now swollen with hotels and nightclubs jammed with reveling Europeans on package tours, modern Bodrum hardly acknowledges its Greek past. The tomb of Mausolos (one of the Seven Wonders of the World and the source of our word "mausoleum") is pretty much a hole in the ground on an out-of-the-way street, its stones having been robbed for other structures, including the medieval Castle of St. Peter at the harbor. Herodotus, who anyway lived before Mausolos, is remembered only in the name of "a busy crossroads with a petrol station on one side."

The few times I have been in Bodrum (which mostly predate the Syrian Civil War, the refugee crisis and the increasing crackdowns of the Erdogan government), I've found it a tourist zoo, a fleecing ground for foreigners with little of the fascination of other Turkish towns. It's nice to rent a boat and go swimming off the coast, but the crowds, the noise, the blaring commercialism of the city are all pretty unbearable. Mary Lee Settle's *Turkish Reflections*, a book that seems to have eluded Marozzi, depicts a more livable Bodrum before mass development.

No one is more disappointed by this cold trail in a hot town than Marozzi, and at least he discovers the most intriguing features of the place—nightclubs for their weirdness and underwater archeology for its riches. The latter provides fascinating arcana about the ancient world, and the journalist in Marozzi rounds up the right people to interview regarding shipwrecks like the *Uluburun*:

> From 1984 to 1994, they unearthed an expanding catalogue of treasures from seven civilizations of the eastern Mediterranean. The *Uluburun* contained products from the Mycenaeans, Canaanites, Cypriots, Egyptians, Kassites, Nubians and Assyrians. The "metal biscuits with ears" were copper ingots shaped like oxhides, the ore for which was almost certainly mined in Cyprus. The cargo contained 354 of them, weighing approximately 10 tons. There was another ton of tin ingots. Mixing the two together would have created enough bronze to equip an entire army.

These landings of submerged artifacts not only have filled two museums in the Castle of St. Peter with objects of spectacular beauty, but also have taught the world about travel and commerce nearly a thousand years before Herodotus. Marozzi's digression, like side trips taken by his subject, reveals an interconnected set of societies, every bit as multicultural as our own.

I suppose you could say the same about the nightclubs:

> Whistles from the dance floor tear into the night. Red lasers shoot across the sky, the bass boom-booms away. Fountains play over lithe professional dancers in postage-stamp bikinis, drenching them as they whip the crowd into a frenzy. A dancer glides on to the stage, long blonde hair and tiny thong, acres of naked skin glistening in the lights. The throbbing dance floor cheers as one and whistles rise into a crescendo as she slinks towards a cannon pointing at the party.

It's not only the clichés in Marozzi's prose that give one pause—what else could a crowd be whipped into but a frenzy?—but also the idiocy of the human behavior. The cannon ejaculates foam on the whole crowd, engendering more Dionysian play. Frankly, I'd rather be undersea.

But Marozzi is on to something: these observations of human ritual are precisely the sort of thing Herodotus would have loved, perhaps in part because he knew the worst sides of human interaction as well as the best. He knew war. When Marozzi travels to Iraq, hoping to find a semblance of the Babylon Herodotus may or may not have seen, his book becomes an indictment of George W. Bush's policies. "No one is fool enough to choose war instead of peace," said Herodotus, but the "Coalition of the Willing" did precisely that. Marozzi found himself at the Baghdad airport in July 2004, when the road into the city was frequently cut by ambushes and roadside bombs of a mounting insurgency.

> All the elements of the war in Iraq carried an unmistakably Herodotean echo: they sounded the enduring themes of empire, imperial over-reach, the sensible limits of power, cultural confrontation and the clash of civilizations, democracy versus dictatorship, West versus East, religion, greed, hubris and its consequences.

The strung-together clichés of this passage might be part of its point. History can seem a bombardment of human stupidities. Others have noted that a reading of Thucydides, who saw Athenian democracy ground down by the Peloponnesian War, has much to teach America about our own political frailty. Marozzi finds Herodotus' tales of clashes between Persia and the Greeks to be equally apt. He produces especially frightening evidence of the way evangelical Christianity has taken hold of our armed forces, and compares American paranoia about Islam to the madness of Cambyses, the Persian king who desecrated Egyptian tombs. Such vilification of "the other" is a human universal. But whatever else we can say about multiculturalism, which has turned some liberal thinkers into waffling relativists, it is certainly a more successful strategy than Bush's blunderings in a war we had many good reasons—including international law—to avoid.

The site of ancient Babylon was trashed by Coalition forces with no regard for history, but Marozzi points out that Saddam had already turned the place into a sort of Disneyland with his inept reconstruction of monuments:

> Nebuchadnezzar made his mark with stunning, convention-challenging architecture which defied technology and awed the world. Saddam's approach was simpler. Rebuild on top of whatever ruins remained, make a new city and don't worry about what the original incarnation looked like.

Shades of "Ozymandias." The sheer insanity of what he describes is also quintessentially Herodotean—and, alas, human. What a species of egomaniacal nutcakes we are, driven by religious zealotry, fantasies of grandeur, and the basic (not to say baser) instincts. It's a wonder we've ever done anything good.

The journey to Egypt proves easier on the soul, with its images (all before the "Arab Spring") of a civil people, river culture, the arcana of embalming, and some Hollywood associations (much to do with Count László de Almásy and the movie version of Michael Ondaatje's novel, *The English Patient*). But Marozzi reserves the latter half of his book for the location toward which he has tended from the beginning, peninsular and island Greece, the modern home of what are essentially still the language and the people of Herodotus. For many of us this is more familiar territory, surveyed here with journalistic skill, including such phenomena as the Junta, the protests of November 17, 1973, and the Papandreou scandals of the 1990s as well as the fraught relationship of contemporary Greeks to manifestations of their ancient past. (The global economic crises beginning in 2008 were too recent to make it into his book, but would have provided fascinating material.) Herodotus becomes the father of sane political philosophy, an advocate for endangered democratic principles.

Two passages from the Greek chapters prove particularly memorable. One describes the ancient tunnel built by Eupalinos on the island of Samos. A feat of engineering intended to bring water to the town from the spring of Ayades in the north, the tunnel still astonishes because it was dug (and reinforced) from two directions at once. No one can quite be sure how its engineers were able to make the ends meet without modern surveying instruments. The tunnel of Eupalinos becomes Marozzi's metaphor for the connectedness of Herodotus' *Histories* and his own book—an intriguing mystery, a blind groping ultimately leading to a useful and happy meeting.

The second memorable passage is a chapter about a lunch with yet another inspiriting figure, Patrick Leigh Fermor, whom Marozzi sees as a modern inheritor of the Herodotean tradition. Yet, like most of us who know anything at all about Paddy (and I have known him since 1980), Marozzi is in awe both of his military deeds and his literary gifts, so his encounter hardly gets beyond the legendary aspects of the man.

I last saw Paddy about a year ago. He was 93 at the time, still a marvel of memory. Introducing Paddy to Americans readers still takes a bit of doing—rather like putting Byron himself into context. Essentially he is famous for three things: helping in World War II to kidnap General Heinrich Kreipe, the German commander of Crete; building an extraordinary stone villa into a point of land in southern Greece; and writing some of the most intoxicating English prose of the last century. If you don't know Leigh Fermor's books, you're missing out. You can't rush them. Give yourself time to reread his beguiling sentences and you will find they far exceed what the marketers call "travel writing." His works include two essential books about Greece, *Mani* and *Roumeli*, two volumes of a projected (and longed-for) trilogy about his youthful walk across Europe, *A Time of Gifts* and *Between the Woods and the Water*, a lovely short book about monasteries, and a few other titles. One good introduction to Paddy's oeuvre is *Words of Mercury*, edited by his biographer, Artemis Cooper, which has the advantage of gathering stuff you can't find elsewhere, including pieces demonstrating Paddy's prowess as a nonsense writer.

To me he has always been the preeminent example of a life lived on its own terms, unhampered by demands of career, etc. The war had given him enough reality, you might say, and the villa afforded him a place to hunker down and indulge his imaginative side. I won't claim he's everybody's cup of tea or shot of ouzo—some find him too aristocratic or just don't "get" his open-armed, Herodotean embrace of experience—but for my money no one has written better than Paddy about the places where history, imagination, and travel meet.

The novelty of all this to Marozzi makes his chapter a good introduction for the uninitiated to Paddy, his villa, and his books. Herodotus had to reconstruct a world on scant evidence, he says. "Leigh Fermor did much the same in *A Time of Gifts*, published in 1977, more than forty years after his original journey across Europe. It was 'like reconstructing a brontosaur from half an eye socket and a basket full of bones,' he wrote of the demands it made on his memory. In some instances, he resorted to creative writing. Not unlike our Greek historian, perhaps." Creative or not, Paddy's reconstructions of a world before the war are gorgeously appointed, and few doubt the uncanny reach of his memory. An acquaintance in Greece has just emailed me, "I'll give Paddy your salutations the next time he pauses from quoting—the last time it was hundreds of lines from a Roman-Etruscan showdown epic by Macauley."

In America, fans of Paddy's books are something of a secret club. We have a handshake and an ouzo toast and accept with quiet resignation that we might never see the final volume of his trilogy. In the meantime we have been appeased by new volumes of letters and other writings. The latest collection of letters, published in 2008 by John Murray, the venerable house that gave us Byron as well as all of Paddy's books, is *In Tearing Haste: Letters Between Deborah Devonshire and Patrick Leigh Fermor*. Fairly dripping with English eccentricity, the book is not only an ebullient addition to Paddy's canon, but also a revealing look at some of history's side currents—English aristocracy of the last sixty years and the life of an expatriate author.

Deborah, Duchess of Devonshire—called Debo throughout the book—is the youngest of the Mitford sisters (including writers Nancy and Jessica and Nazi sympathizer Diana). Married to the late Andrew Cavendish, she has lived much of her life at Chatsworth and at Lismore Castle in Ireland. She comes across as the epitome of the no-nonsense English noblewoman, frank and funny, without a sentimental bone in her body. One photograph shows her on a shooting party, ejected shotgun shells caught mid-air as if fired from her steely gaze. She claims to detest reading books. The only things she shares with Paddy are her class and her apolitical nature. In fact, she is amused by the legends surrounding him, as she says in a brief introductory note: "For eighteen months, Paddy and his great friend Xan Fielding lived in the mountains of Crete disguised as shepherds (I wouldn't put him in charge of my sheep, but never mind). . . ."

They first saw each other before the war, eventually married others (Paddy's wife, Joan, died in 2003), and have remained loyal to each other over the years, sometimes visiting each other's houses, sometimes reporting from excursions abroad. Their lives appear like something most of us experience only in books and movies—no one mentions money, for example—but they make very amusing company, and in places Paddy's writing rises to the level of his best. His whimsicality is on show from the start, when he responds to Debo's invitation to Ireland, writing from a friend's home in Greece:

> My plan is this: there is a brilliant young witch on this island (aged sixteen and very pretty), sovereign at thwarting the evil eye, casting out devils and foiling spells by incantation. It shouldn't be beyond her powers to turn me into a fish for a month and slip me into the harbour. I reckon I could get through the Mediterranean, across the Bay of Biscay, round Land's End and over the Irish Sea in about 28 days (if the weather holds) and on into the Blackwater. I'm told there's a stream that flows under your window, up which I propose to swim and, with a final effort, clear the sill and land on the carpet, where I insist on being treated like the frog prince for a couple of days of rest and recovery. (You could have a tank brought up—or lend me your bath if this is not inconvenient—till I'm ready to come downstairs. Also, some flannel trousers, sensible walking shoes and a Donegal tweed Norfolk jacket with a belt across the small of the back and leather buttons.) But please be there. Otherwise, there is all the risk of filleting, *meunière*, etc, and worst of all, *au bleu* . . .

It's a life of inspired insouciance, punctuated by hangovers, fox hunts, meals, expeditions, and a few political intrusions. Debo's letters are usually short and to the point, while Paddy's are flights and divagations, meanderings, waxings. Like Herodotus they have both known war and are left with a heavy dose of fatalism's epicurean compensations. The good meal among friends is the truly important encounter, even when it leaves Paddy vowing to give up cigarettes and alcohol.

Early on we find him on the set of *Ill Met by Moonlight*, the movie about his exploits on Crete (he was played as a jolly schoolboy soldier by Dirk Bogarde). Nothing in the movie rings true to him, but he can't resist having fun with the actors and crew (I finally found the film on YouTube and judge it not bad at all). Later, he has alarming encounters with Americans in Paris: "I am writing this in the mosaic courtyard of this luxurious hotel, with a bogus Spanish fountain tinkling in the middle. The Frogs and Americans here look awful, exactly like pigs, with tiny pig's eyes. I have just caught a sobering glimpse of my own reflection, and so, alas, do I. Circe has done a thorough job." This occurs after a meeting with the film producer Darryl Zanuck, who hired Paddy to adapt Romain Gary's novel, *The Roots of Heaven*, for the screen. American bluntness has a perplexing effect on Paddy, as he adds in a later reflection about a meeting in London:

> I deposited the "treatment," as agreed, for Darryl Zanuck at the Savoy. Next morning I turned up at his suite, which was full of smoke. "Come in, Mr. Fermor," he said, "sit down." He puffed at his cigar in silence. I asked him if he had got the treatment. After a few more silent puffs he said, "it's a whole heap of crap," then, after another pause, he said, "IT'S NO GOOD!" There was a further pause, and several puffs. Oddly enough I felt rather relieved. It wasn't my world, after all. But after more silence and several puffs, he said, "We're going to the races." I looked a bit puzzled, so he went on. "We go to Paris tomorrow and I'll get you a suite like mine in the Hôtel Prince de Galles and a bottle of whisky and a nice-looking typist, and we'll get down to it. Is your passport OK for French Equatorial Africa?"

I have not seen *The Roots of Heaven* since watching it in high school on a neighbor's TV. At the time I thought it exalting, but the years and the critics have not been kind. Paddy remained ambivalent about the project—perhaps his manners and literary refinement were no match for the bluster of Zanuck and his director, John Huston. He loved Trevor Howard and Errol Flynn and adored Juliette Gréco (but could not comprehend her affair with Zanuck). "On the whole," he wrote Debo, "with one or two exceptions—apart from those mentioned—I hate the lot of them. The standard of conversation and jokes is deplorable, and sometimes I feel on the brink of weeping."

Paddy's boyish soul can hardly bear the modern world, so he moves through it from one island of civility to another. He got enough reality in the war, so civilized friendship has a saving power for him. He's not one for introspection or autobiography, and the poetry in his prose derives from his outward look, his embrace of others.

Debo's marriage did not prevent her from developing crushes on others as well. One was for Xan Fielding, whom I met in 1980—a dashing figure with a past as unconventional as Paddy's. Another Debo crush was on Jack Kennedy. She attended his inauguration in 1961 and found him captivating. This book gives us Paddy's short letter about JFK's death, concluding, "What a beastly age to live in." Then Debo's report of December 1963: "We went to Washington for his funeral. Oh it was strange, Americans aren't suited to tragedy. They like everything to be great. I was more or less alright in church till his friends came in & their crumpled miserable faces were too much & it was floods all the way after that." Tenacious ebullience and the stiff upper lip prove vulnerable, even in this buoyant book.

There is much more to be said about it—the great depictions of travels in Greece, Peru, and the Himalayas, the passing of friends of their beloved spouses, the onset of old age with its tragicomic distortions. But I want to end with Paddy's first description of a piece of land, Kalamitsi, in Greece. The letter is dated August 1962:

Darling Debo,

I've spent the last two months trying to find somewhere to live in S. W. Greece, and, the trouble is, I've found it; trouble, because I don't think we'll be able to get it; owned by too many people, scattered all over the globe, who, though none of them live there, are unlikely to want to sell it; but I live on hopes. It's in the Mani, a peninsula in the middle of a steep deserted bay, pointing S. E., E., S. W., and W., with a great amphitheatre of mountains which turn a hectic red at sunset. The peninsula descends like a giant, shallow staircase of olive groves, plumed with cypress trees, platform after platform dwindling to a low cliff thirty feet above deep blue-green glittering sea, with trees and wild sweet-smelling shrubs to the very brim, full of beehives, olives, woodpigeons and with a freshwater spring.

I know that land. I lived there in a stone hut for six months in 1981. By that time, Paddy had long since inhabited his great villa in a beautiful walled compound on an adjacent property. My "landlord" in those days—one owner of the land Paddy had wanted to buy—was an aged Greek just returned from a lifetime making money in America, and I spent a lot of my time disobeying his orders to cut down trees. Instead, in lieu of rent, I worked to improve the little hut, painting its walls with lime, fixing the door and a rustic bed, putting screens on the two windows. I learned how to grow vegetables from a lovely couple named Petros and Lela, who worked for Paddy and Joan. My garden was fed by the freshwater spring, which is now completely obscured by a mound of brambles.

These days Mani bustles with tourists. Other houses have crowded into Kalamitsi, and Paddy endures the regular onslaught of visitors like Justin Marozzi and me. We all want to be a part of what he has made. Sitting on one of his terraces at the edge of the sea, hearing the waves washing the rocks below and the blackbirds twittering in the garden, one can indeed feel touched by timeless journeys and the stout-hearted people who made them and wrote them down. One feels connected not to a better world, but to a better version of the one we have. A story.

2010

The Silk Road of Poetry

OMAR KHAYYAM AND
EDWARD FITZGERALD

ONE OF THE MOST SUCCESSFUL poetry books of all time, *The Rubaiyat of Omar Khayyam* nearly went undiscovered and unread. A young philologist, Whitley Stokes, noticed the 34-page collection of English quatrains in a remainder bin in 1861. It had been published two years earlier and claimed to be a translation of poems by the "Astronomer-Poet of Persia." Stokes bought the unsold copies and passed them on to friends, including Dante Gabriel Rossetti. Then, according to Robert Richardson in *Nearer the Heart's Desire*, his elegant dual biography of Khayyam and his translator, "Rossetti showed the *Rubaiyat* to Algernon Swinburne, who was twenty-four at the time, and soon the poem was known to George Meredith, age twenty-three, to William Morris, age twenty-seven, to Edward Burne-Jones, then twenty-eight, and to John Ruskin, then forty-two. None of them knew who the translator was." He was Edward FitzGerald, "a bohemian scholar-gypsy masquerading as a Victorian gentleman," in Mr. Richardson's words, and one of the more eccentric literary figures of the 19th century.

Word of mouth and a few influential reviews made the book a publishing phenomenon. "By 1929," Richardson notes, "there had been 586 English editions of FitzGerald's *Rubaiyat*. It has been translated into at least fifty-four languages, and most of the translations are from FitzGerald, not from the original Persian." Perhaps in all of literary history there exists no book in which translator and original author are so hard to tell apart. Khayyam was a substantial scientist and philosopher in 11th-century Persia, and nearly a millennium later FitzGerald produced other translations from Spanish and Greek. But we remember them both for this one small volume.

Not so long ago, copies of *The Rubaiyat of Omar Khayyam* were found in most literate households, and it was a part of our popular culture. Quatrain 12, one of the most famous stanzas— "*ruba'i* is Persian for quatrain, *rubaiyat* is the plural"—gave Eugene O'Neill the title for his only comedy, *Ah, Wilderness!* (1933) and featured in a *Peanuts* cartoon:

> A Book of Verses underneath the Bough,
> A Jug of Wine, a Loaf of Bread—and Thou
> Beside me singing in the Wilderness—
> Oh, Wilderness were Paradise enow!

Our word "paradise," Richardson notes, derives from the Farsi word for "the walled Persian gardens, the *para daezas*" common to the Seljuq Empire in which Khayyam lived and wrote. Both Victorians and Moderns enjoyed the epicurean nonconformity of these brief poems, with their fatalistic emphasis on drinking and physical pleasure. In a famous poem, Edwin Arlington Robinson's character Mr. Flood quoted a *ruba'i* at his drunken party with the moon. Wallace Stevens owned a copy and was no doubt under its influence when he wrote in "The Snow Man" of "the listener, who listens in the snow, / And, nothing himself, beholds / Nothing that is not there and the nothing that is." Here is the "Rubaiyat's" forty-eighth quatrain:

> A Moment's Halt—a momentary taste
> Of BEING from the Well amid the Waste—
> And Lo!—the phantom Caravan has reach'd
> The NOTHING it set out from—Oh, make haste!

Robert Frost modified the *ruba'i* (rhymed aaba) for his most famous poem "Stopping by Woods on a Snowy Evening." Ezra Pound even named his adopted son Omar after the Persian master.

We know very little about Khayyam, and therein lies half of Richardson's tale. There is no direct textual evidence of Khayyam's verses, editions of which were only compiled a century after his death. What we do know is that he was born in 1048 in what is today northeastern Iran—in Nishapur, an important post on the Silk Road, the trade route that becomes Richardson's metaphor for communication between East and West. During Khayyam's lifetime the Turkic-Persian Seljuqs expanded their empire from the Hindu Kush to Anatolia, and he served at least two great sultans: Alp Arslan and Malik-Shah, "a patron of learning, science, art and literature" at a time when Europe was enduring its Dark Ages. Khayyam was known as a court philosopher and mathematician. His astronomical observations led to a calendar more accurate than the Gregorian version we use now.

"Nishapur was more than a garden city," Richardson writes. "Cloth weavers used locally produced saffron, madder, henna, and indigo for dyes. Sesame oil was more used than olive oil. Dozens of different kinds of melons grew and as many as a hundred different varieties of grapes were grown for the flourishing wine trade. Despite the Islamic ban on alcohol, wine drinking was widespread and it has never had a greater poet than Omar Khayyam." As the seventy-fourth quatrain puts it:

YESTERDAY *This* Day's Madness did prepare;
TO-MORROW's Silence, Triumph, or Despair:
Drink! For you know not whence you came nor why:
Drink! For you know not why you go, nor where.

But it was not just the fevered hedonism of these short poems that endeared them to the world. It was also their anti-authoritarian, anti-puritanical stance and their awareness of the unpredictability of life. In Khayyam's lifetime, the Seljuqs were subject to one of the great revolts within Islam, the time of the Assassins, a Shiite rebellion under the murderous Hasan-i Sabbah. The poetry attributed to Khayyam is opposed to religious fundamentalism, while, according to Richardson, "everything we know about Hasan suggests he believed in a rigid, monolithic absolutism and authoritarianism."

In *Nearer the Heart's Desire*, Richardson emphasizes the pessimism of the *Rubaiyat* and the youth of the book's greatest enthusiasts. "There is something sadly appealing," he writes, "something pleasantly confirming, about our visions of lost empires, ruined cities, and dethroned kings." Part of the appeal, he notes, is Khayyam's answer: "Live all you can. Right now. It's a mistake not to." FitzGerald worked on the *Rubaiyat* during what Richardson calls "the roughest domestic stretch" of his life, while a disastrous marriage was running its short course. One of the miracles is that the poet doesn't "brood over lost time and vanished youth. He loves it, celebrates it, knows it to be all the sweeter for being temporary."

In the early 1850s, a young scholar and linguistic prodigy named Edward Cowell introduced FitzGerald to Persian literature and became one of his most intimate friends. In 1856, Cowell copied out the quatrains attributed to Omar Khayyam that he had found in a manuscript at Oxford and sent them to FitzGerald. Cowell also married Elizabeth Charlesworth—"a vicar's daughter with whom FitzGerald had been half in love for years"—and for a few years the three friends were inseparable. When the Cowells emigrated to India, FitzGerald "felt the loss" as another "catastrophe" on top of his own troubled domestic arrangements. Translating and sequencing the Khayyam poems may have been a way of making sense of life's disappointments. FitzGerald took unconnected quatrains and made a quasi-narrative of a single day, which he described in a letter to his publisher: "He begins with Dawn pretty sober and contemplative; then as he thinks and drinks, grows savage, blasphemous etc. and then again sobers down into melancholy at nightfall." Readers new and old can follow this narrative—or take the poems in any sequence they wish—in a companion edition of the *Rubaiyat* edited by Richardson and subtly and suggestively illustrated by Lincoln Perry's watercolors.

Scholars have labored to determine what in the *Rubaiyat* is Khayyam, what FitzGerald, but "one of the great translations in world literature" will always be cloaked in ambiguity. What is reality, what is romance? When are we reading FitzGerald's allusions to Milton or Blake instead of the tropes of a medieval Persian? For example, quatrain eighty-seven uses the traditional metaphor of potter and pot for creator and creation, but in FitzGerald's version we might more recall Blake's famous "Tyger":

> Whereat some one of the loquacious Lot—
> I think a Sufi pipkin—waxing hot—
> "All this of Pot and Potter—Tell me then,
> Who is the Potter, pray, and who the Pot?"

Most readers today know nothing of Edward FitzGerald. "Who was he really," Richardson asks, "and how had he come to produce his extraordinary book of verses?" From the golden age of Islam, he takes us to Suffolk, England, where Edward FitzGerald was born in 1809, the seventh of eight children in a staggeringly wealthy family. He received a very literary education, and when he entered Trinity College, Cambridge, at seventeen he embraced with body and soul the scholar's life—

including a steady diet of wine and tobacco. He numbered among his friends at university William Makepeace Thackeray and Alfred Tennyson. A more surprising friend, perhaps, was the older Thomas Carlyle. Enthusiasm characterized these friendships. Richardson quotes a FitzGerald letter to charming effect: "I spent one evening with Carlyle, but was very dull somehow, and delighted to get out into the street. An organ was playing a polka even so late in the street: and Carlyle was rather amazed to see me polka down the pavement—He shut his street door—to which he always accompanies you—with a kind of a groan."

Other than his brief marriage, he lived a bachelor's life, devoted to his friends, his translations, and sailing a yacht called Scandal with its dinghy, Whisper. Speculations about his sexuality are inevitable, and Richardson treats them cautiously. In a letter of 1834, FitzGerald wrote: "I am an idle fellow, of a very ladylike turn of sentiment, and my friendships are more like loves, I think." His intellectual loves included not just Omar Khayyam but also the Epicurean poet Lucretius, whose masterpiece, *On the Nature of Things*, has been so influential on our more skeptical philosophers. "Lucretius is strong medicine," Richardson writes. "Gods exist, but they live in a world apart from ours and have nothing to do with us. Lucretius' cold-eyed conclusion is that we are not now and we have never been worth a moment's notice from them. . . . Worshipping gods is not only foolish, it is wrong and leads to evil." The balancing motive of this worldview is love, which at its best expects nothing in return. Richardson, who has made a distinguished career as an intellectual biographer of figures like William James and Emerson, writes sympathetically of these connections: "John Ruskin said one's work should be the praise of what one loves. This is true for Lucretius, who loved the work of Epicurus; it is true for FitzGerald, who loved the work of Omar Khayyam; and it is true for those who have loved the work of Edward FitzGerald."

Love has inspired Richardson's book, too, which begins with memories of his father, a lawyer who knew the whole poetic sequence by heart. Perhaps the *Rubaiyat* is a sort of wisdom book as much as a sequence of poems. Perhaps it really is a Silk Road of the imagination.

The Unseeable,
Unsayable World

IN ISTANBUL IN 1924, an American went looking for a grave.
He had met the sultan of the now-dead Ottoman Empire, who
lived exiled in Italy, and had heard about a complicated man
from the east, Jamal al-Din al-Afghani, a major thinker about
the place of Muslim people in the world, and now in the new
Turkey he wandered the cemeteries searching for the great
man's remains. It was an unmarked grave.

The American was Charles Crane, a wealthy philanthropist
with a passion for Islamic culture, and he thought al-Afghani
deserved a proper tomb. His search would have proved fruit-
less, Pankaj Mishra writes in *From the Ruins of Empire*, but for
a lucky meeting with "a distinguished-looking Muslim man in
a green turban" who offered to show him the burial site. This
man remembered the right cemetery and the grave's location
in line with two trees.

Was it al-Afghani, "one of the most distinguished Muslims
that ever lived"? If so, why did this fervent intellectual, born in
Persia but ironically associated with Afghanistan, end his days

obscurely in a corrupt, dying empire? Crane believed what he was told and paid for a monument to be erected on the spot.

In the Muslim world the name of al-Afghani had never died out. His writings and his reputation remained influential among all pan-Arabist thinkers and critics of Western imperialism. Though he had once been imprisoned in Afghanistan, that country claimed him as a son, and in 1944 his body—if indeed it was his body—was flown to Karachi, trained to Peshawar, and transported by road to Kabul.

All along the route al-Afghani's remains were met by crowds. And when the hero was "reburied on the grounds of Kabul University," dignitaries from across the world were on hand. As Mishra writes in his ambitious, jam-packed history of modern Asian intellectuals, "Potentates and poets vied to hail the Muslim leader as Afghanistan's most distinguished son (carefully avoiding Tehran's objections that al-Afghani was actually Persian by birth). The British, the Americans, and the Russians laid wreaths on the grave. The German ambassador gave a Nazi salute."

Mishra's book teems with such ironies. Even my effort to write about it is, in an odd way, symptomatic of the situation. Of the three central figures in this "group portrait"—al-Afghani, China's Liang Qichao, and India's Rabindranath Tagore—I had only known the Nobel Prize-winning poet, Tagore, in any depth. Dozens of thinkers, radicals, poets, and politicians are discussed in this book, but those three are its dramatic focus—a helpful geometry because so much information is rammed into fewer than 400 pages. Before I say anything about the strengths and weaknesses of Mishra's endeavor, I must point out its obvious importance as an introduction for Western readers, at least readers like me, to vast tracts of hitherto unknown intellectual life. As a child of the sixties I grew up hearing constantly about many other figures Mishra discusses, from Sun Yat-Sen to Ho Chi Minh and Frantz Fanon, but it would never have occurred to me that these lives and ideas from so many disparate parts of the globe could be brought together in a single synthetic postcolonial study. Probably they can't—at least without oversimplifying all kinds of complicated motives, collisions, collusions, and catastrophes, but Mishra endeavors against all odds and manages some convincing comparisons.

What unites these three figures is principally their reaction against Western imperialism, but Mishra's study, while packed with anguished dissidents, is not in itself a shrill polemic. It is foremost a set of related stories, the "result of serendipitous reading," as he says in his "Bibliographic Essay" at the back. He credits earlier historians pointing to Western ignorance of Asian thought, adding, "This ignorance . . . was also widespread among Asians themselves, especially those brought up, like myself, on histories of nation-building."

I should also note the difficulties inherent in the word "Asian," which in this case means anything from Istanbul and Egypt east, excluding Russia, here associated with the imperial structures of Europe. Right away, one can raise objections—is it the Bosporus you intend as a border, and isn't that a rather arbitrary designation even within that great city, rife with so much that is Western, so much that is not? And how does one distinguish Egypt from so much else in North Africa, and indeed sub-Saharan Africa? Mishra clearly has to beg our indulgence of any number of slights and generalizations in order to make his history work. So grant it to him and get on with it.

From the Ruins of Empire is a useful book, but it is also an exhausting one, its pages laden with so much detail, so many names, allusions, quotations, that it is sometimes hard to apprehend the shape and purpose of the whole. It must have been a real headache to write. Mishra has so many constituencies to elucidate, so much geography to cover, and he does it with relative brevity. Compare this to the nearly six hundred pages Peter Hopkirk lavished on *The Great Game* (1992), his spellbinding account of Russian and British intrigue mostly in Afghanistan.

Like Hopkirk's, Mishra's book is best when he tells stories, and his first major character, al-Afghani, quickly becomes a fascinating figure for his contradictions. A thinker, writer, political activist without country or portfolio, al-Afghani was just about everywhere—from India and Central Asia to Egypt, Europe and Russia. He was born in the late 1830s and died in 1897, and while he apparently grew up in a Shi'a household he later claimed Afghan heritage to appeal to the Sunni majority in the Arab world. He was a foundational thinker in the pan-Islamic movement seeking to counter the global dominance of the Western powers. Fair enough. Pan-Islamism is an identity movement without a nationalist bent such as one feels in the Celtic Revival in Ireland. Identity movements define themselves not only by the positive attributes of a given culture, but also in opposition to a perceived *other*, a power culture or outsider empire. What's fascinating about al-Afghani is his protean development, the way his thinking adapted to and evolved with his times and circumstances. He was a brilliant, sensitive man who could see wrong in many quarters and thought acutely about it.

In 1868 al-Afghani was in Kabul fomenting anti-British sentiments, trying to influence the amir, Sher Ali. But Sher Ali made other calculations, including a rapprochement with England that forced al-Afghani into exile. Mishra writes, "Imprisoned at the Bala Hisar fort in Kabul awaiting expulsion from the country, he composed in rhymed prose an ironic commentary on the misunderstandings he evoked in Afghanistan (and would soon evoke in many other countries)." This text is worth quoting in full, not only for what it reveals about its author's personal state, but also for what it shows about the obstacles he faced within and without the Islamic world:

The English people believe me a Russian
The Muslims think me a Zoroastrian
The Sunnis think me an enemy of Ali

Some of the friends of the four companions have believed me
    a Wahhabi
Some of the virtuous Imamites have imagined me a Babi
The theists have imagined me a materialist
And the pious a sinner bereft of piety
the learned have considered me an unknowing ignoramus
And the believers have thought me an unbelieving sinner
Neither does the unbeliever call me to him
Nor the Muslim recognize me as his own
Banished from the mosque and rejected from the temple
I am perplexed as to whom I should depend on and whom I should
    fight
The rejection of one makes the friends firm against the opposite
There is no way of escape for me to flee the grasp of the one group
There is no fixed abode for me to fight the other party
Seated in Bala Hisar in Kabul, my hands tied and my legs
Broken, I want to see what the Curtain of the Unknown will
Deign to reveal to me and what fate the turning of this malevolent
Firmament has in store for me.

His strength and his problem were that he was both a believer
and a modernizer, trying to speak in a world where his own
people could be suspicious, to say the least, of secular thinking,
and where Europeans looked down on him for the very color
of his skin. Mind you, the dismissive attitudes of religious fun-
damentalists have never been a solely Islamic phenomenon. I
just saw a news report stating that more than fifty per cent of
Americans believe God rewards people who pray. These kinds
of delusions appear to be a human universal.

    It would be wrong to say al-Afghani encountered no sym-
pathetic Europeans in his "strange odyssey." Yet he struggled
against intolerance, whether it came from Western imperial-
ists or Eastern despotism, from blinkered intellectuals or religious zealots. He believed in a rational Islam, and favored
women's rights. One of his few romantic entanglements ap-

pears to have been with a German woman at a time when he had temporarily adopted European dress—just try untangling all the twisted threads in that! And he engaged in a public debate with the French philosopher Ernest Renan about Islam and science—a widely-disseminated exchange soured not only by Renan's prejudices, but also by al-Afghani's perception that he could not be perceived to say anything against religion. It was impossible to say just what he meant without offending either Christian readers or Muslim ones. If he wasn't careful he could lose credibility among the very people he sought to liberate.

In many parts of the world these subjugated people suffered terribly, with few rights and opportunities. When anti-imperial rebellions broke out, such as that of the Mahdi in the Sudan, culminating in the 1885 massacre at Khartoum, al-Afghani could see the utility of killing. "He never ceased to quote the Koranic verse, 'God does not change the condition of a people until they change their own condition.'" Not much help, that. He was not a pacifist like Gandhi, though the inevitability of violence tormented him. Forces arrayed against ordinary Muslim people—autocratic rulers, intolerance, economic barriers, racism and ignorance on all sides—must have appeared insurmountable. There were occasions, such as the brutal British reaction to the 1857 Sepoy Mutiny (Indian people prefer to call it the First War of Liberation), which could only be met by outrage.

Make an epic film about Gandhi and inevitably he will come out a saint, no matter his foibles. The epic of al-Afghani would be rife with tragic ironies. How can we reconcile his belief in "the essential unity of the great monotheistic religions," his rejection of "the Shiite-Sunni schism" in Islam, his belief in "the necessity of constitutional reforms," with his revolutionary rage? Furthermore, how can we not be appalled at his influence on later forms of tyranny, such as the Iranian Revolution of the late 1970s and its subsequent state (cf. Azar Nafisi's *Reading Lolita in Tehran*)? Who knows where new freedom movements like the Arab Spring are heading, whether to real democracies or other forms of government that protect vulnerable people, or to new forms of despotism and exploitation? Al-Afghani is one of the intellectuals contributing to such foment, and Mishra's book gets some of its power from the ongoing turmoil of our present world. A great writer or filmmaker could fashion a drama of Shakespearean magnitude out of such material.

One further irony. In 2002, following the initial defeat of the Taliban in Afghanistan, the United States pledged $25,000 to restore al-Afghani's tomb, which had been damaged in that country's perpetual wars. Repairs were completed in 2010. One wonders whether the tomb will remain safe from further on-slaughts in that "grave of empires." One also wonders whose bones are really interred there.

No RELIGIOUS OR POLITICAL THINKER of a given era can pre-dict the uses to which his thought will be put in the future. Jesus and Mohammed lived as they lived, and look what great and horrible things have been done in their names. Karl Marx lived as he lived, thought as he thought, and look at what the human species has often made of him. Because Pankaj Mishra has written a novel and a history of Buddhism as well as the present book, I found myself wondering what his vision was of human interaction. Does he really believe in progress or that conflict can be eliminated? What is the place of any theory of melioration in the story of mankind? As his book demon-strates, ideas can be necessary and dangerous at the same time.

Yet al-Afghani cannot be blamed for the ideas of the Aya-tollah Khomeini or Osama bin Laden any more than Ameri-can founders could have predicted the absurd proportions of gun ownership in the present day or the vast, soulless and alienating commercialism so many of us live with now. What becomes clear in Mishra's book, as one pushes through the blizzard of detail and begins to see the larger picture, is that he is interested in understanding and clarifying the current situation more than judging it. That seems utterly commendable. But the reality of the situation, such as it is, could only really be caught by imaginative writers, novelists or dramatists or poets, most of whom seem unwilling or unable to take up the challenge. Mishra clearly has more work cut out for him.

When he moves into the twentieth century he keeps one eye glancing sidelong at developments in the Muslim world, but also takes in China, India, and Japan. The Japanese victory over the Russian navy at the Battle of Tsushima in 1905 indicated one kind of choice available to emerging Asian countries—a race to modern industrialization fueled by insane nationalism—no nationality, it would seem, has cornered the market on insanity, and there's still plenty of it to go around. Japan's earlier humiliation by the West resulted in violent revenge, not only on the United States and Great Britain, but also on China. Perhaps psychology is as important as history here, since humiliation was also a motive behind the rise of Nazism in Germany. The result we all know. Being Asian or European wasn't the issue. Being human was—and human beings are capable of utter madness, utter stupidity, utter destruction.

In the case of China and India, a rush to industrialization was not possible. The weight of tradition, the relative passivity of Confucianism and Hinduism, seem to have been part of this, as well as the heavy thumb of Western imperialism that held people down and kept them from prospering. The Chinese scholar, journalist, and reformer Liang Qichao (1873–1929) grew up in the wake of the second Opium War and was a teenager during the Boxer Rebellion. He saw the demise of the Qing Dynasty, the furtive rise of republicanism, the nasty and unpredictable power of the warlords. For his generation, Europe's self-destruction in World War I offered a kind of hope. All eyes turned to Versailles in 1919, where so much of the world's fate would be decided.

The new player on the international stage was the United States, and people from many different nations looked to its apparently idealistic president, Woodrow Wilson, for a way forward. Would the old imperial structures be allowed to remain in place, would Europe and the new Soviet state carve up the rest of the world, or would the colonized peoples of the world have any say? "Liang was at least part of an official delegation certain of representation at the conference, unlike many others—the Iranians, the Syrians and the Armenians—who tried to have their voices heard and were completely rebuffed." So many of the major players in the bloody history of the twentieth century, so many of the ideals that would lead to disastrous wars, were present at Versailles. Ho Chi Minh was hoping to meet Wilson. Tagore admired Wilson's vision and intended to dedicate a book to him. He would be disappointed at how little changed. 1919 was also the year of the Amritsar Massacre, in which British troops killed some three hundred unarmed protestors, another indication of how far Tagore's country still had to go, and even independence would not put an end to violence.

Woodrow Wilson had his own limitations. Mishra suggests that his strain of Southern racism prevented him from seeing many of the people looking to him for help. Then there was the weary cynicism of Europe, which had after all borne the brunt of the destruction (albeit with all kinds of colonial troops pressed to the slaughter). "Wilson's Fourteen Points would have been lofty ideals at any time (God, as the French prime minister Clemenceau joked, had only ten). They were particularly unrealistic during a global war that would soon end with Britain, France and Japan adding to their possessions in the Middle East, Africa and East Asia."

Mishra is good at letting us see the simultaneity of multiple responses to Versailles from all over the world. Watching from China, the twenty-five-year-old Mao Zedong wrote,

Wilson in Paris was like an ant on a hot skillet. He didn't know what to do. He was surrounded by thieves like Clemenceau, Lloyd George, Makino, and Orlando. He heard nothing except accounts of receiving certain amounts of territory and of reparations worth so much in gold. He did nothing except to attend various kinds of meetings where he could not speak his mind. One day a Reuters telegram read, 'President Wilson has finally agreed with Clemenceau's view that Germany not be admitted to the League of Nations.' When I saw the words 'finally agreed', I felt sorry for him for a long time. Poor Wilson!

You know things are bad when Mao becomes the grown-up almost at the table. Europe and America would be no help to the subjugated peoples of Asia. Turkey, which had backed the losing side in the first World War, would stay out of the second and lose access by doing so, but would eventually build a viable secular state in the Muslim world (now, of course, endangered by religious fundamentalism and authoritarian politics). The Middle East was carved up along lines that created myriad problems, again naively misread by the United States in its recent wars. China and Southeast Asia would look to another model, Communism. In the vacuum created by Western powers, the Soviet Union stepped in with its own anti-imperialist challenge, and the so-called Cold War was off and running even before the hot wars had been blown out by a mushroom cloud.

In the wake of his political disappointment at Versailles, Liang's thinking returned to Chinese traditions like Confucianism. Perhaps the way forward could be found through spirituality. He befriended the Indian writer, Tagore, and hosted him in China. Neither figure would live to see any change in the fate of his country.

Rabindranath Tagore (1861–1941) was a poet and novelist who gave lectures throughout the world on the plight of Asia. Tagore had grown up in a wealthy Calcutta family, with all the benefits of a Western-style university education. He believed not only in what he called spirituality as a progressive mode, but also in secular learning. The school he founded in Bengal would eventually train the great filmmaker Satyajit Ray and the economist Amartya Sen. Tagore held that the West needn't be imitated in order for the East to find itself: "The conflict with Europe is waking up all civilized Asia. Asia today is set to realizing herself consciously, and thence with vigour. She has understood, know thyself—that is the road to freedom. In imitating others is destruction."

One may wonder at another form of idealism here, since he is quoting the Greek aphorism from the Temple of Apollo at Delphi, but Tagore had a point. His thinking presented an important strain in the modern struggle—a pacifist identity politics that would align with thinkers from Gandhi to Martin Luther King, Jr. Tagore saw the destructive nature of modern nationalism. He saw what it was doing to Japan, and correctly predicted it would not end well. In his 1968 Nobel lecture, Japanese novelist Yasunari Kawabata would remember seeing Tagore:

> ... with his long bushy hair, long mustache and beard, standing tall in loose-flowing Indian garments, and with deep, piercing eyes. His white hair flowed softly down both sides of his forehead; the tufts of hair under the temples also were like two beards and linking up with the hair on his cheeks, continued into his beard, so that he gave an impression, to the boy that I was then, of some ancient Oriental wizard.

Perhaps it is as a wizard, an artist, that Tagore will have left his most important contribution, yet his global travels and speeches had their importance at the time. Stepping back from history in the final pages of his book, Mishra wonders at the impact of these intellectuals on the world we inhabit today:

> Personally powerless, they lurched between hope and despair, vigorous commitment and a sense of futility. Still, there is a

striking unity to be observed in their perceptions, and this is because as traditionalists or iconoclastic radicals, these thinkers and activists were struggling to articulate a satisfying answer to the same question: how to reconcile themselves and others to the dwindling of their civilization through internal decay and Westernization while regaining parity and dignity in the eyes of the white rulers of the world.

Ultimately, one is confronted with one's own fears and prejudices. My own feeling is that no race, religion, or nationality can be said to have a monopoly on evil, or even error. We can acknowledge the horrors bursting out of these confrontations, the dictatorships and religious fanaticism, the vast scale of modern slaughter, terrorism, etc., and perhaps we can see them as, under the circumstances, inevitable.

On 9/11, I was in Athens, and I remember the gravity of it, the grim churning sensation at the pit of my stomach. I also remembering thinking, "Of course this would happen. Of course it would. Given the nature of things, it was inevitable that such a thing would occur." The hope that we might magically avoid evil, whether from the West or the East, might be the most futile thing of all. Mishra saves his last sobering words to question the "war on terror" and the assumption that people should want to live as Americans do. I think he is right in this, just as he is right to remind us of the killings perpetrated by "Asians" on their own people.

What is missing from his book is the tragic vision of the artist, the recognition that human motives do not really change, only adapt to historical circumstances. In some ways, the dualism of East and West may prove a too-convenient fiction, though I know from experience how strange, how disorienting it can be to move between vastly different cultures. Mishra has found a number of remarkable figures whose ideas helped shape the world we find ourselves in now, and his staggeringly ambitious project is to connect them as nobody before has quite managed to do. This is a necessary step in understanding not only our differences, but also our common humanity. Perhaps what we really need most are artists of Sophoclean or Shakespearean breadth and penetration who can help us understand our contradictory nature and the nature of the world in which we live.

2013

Reading Greece

Awake! (not Greece—she is awake!)
Thy life-blood tracks its parent lake,
Awake my spirit! Think through *whom*
And then strike home.

    —GEORGE GORDON, LORD BYRON

Where is the truth?
I too was an archer in the war;
my fate, that of a man who erred.

    —GEORGE SEFERIS

CULTURES MISREAD EACH OTHER, just as individuals do. It's hard enough—perhaps impossible—to know oneself, as Plato advised, let alone to know another. That doesn't mean we shouldn't try. The whole field of postcolonial literature, which could encompass most literatures of the modern world, arises at points of change that complicate our knowledge; empires recede, new nations clamor for recognition, and individuals live at this busy intersection of tradition and modernity, communal identity invaded by a belief in individual freedom. Though its nature varies from culture to culture, this perceptual intersection can be found at any geographical point in the world. It is an essential reality of life on our planet at the present time, in which most international or inter-cultural conflicts can be understood in postcolonial terms. As I've said elsewhere, only the most reductive studies of these phenomena blame the West and its empires for all the world's troubles and misreadings; the East is equally culpable, and honest investigation reveals that all human beings are caught in this web to greater or lesser degrees. This is one of the problems of being human, and one of the reasons that no human being lives outside history.

Having made these broad assertions, I turn to the specific case of Greece, which has at times been thought of as a sort of transitional point between East and West. What would it mean to *know* Greece, or to represent Greece accurately in literature? Why should anyone care about this tiny modern nation whose language is spoken by relatively few non-Greeks and whose ancient currency, the drachma, has just been replaced by the euro?

What is Greece? What borders in time and space do we use to comprehend it? Do we start with the ancient world, Alexander the Great, Byzantium, the four hundred years of Ottoman domination? Do we use the borders established at independence in 1829, or 1833 when the fledgling monarchy was formally recognized? Those of the Balkan War of 1912–13? The Treaty of Sèvres in 1920? The Asia Minor catastrophe of 1922? Along with the geopolitical reality of its present borders (smaller than the state of Alabama) and its advocacy of border stability in the Balkans, this nation of ten million people remains a cultural presence in Cyprus, Istanbul, Jerusalem, and the global diaspora. Remember El Greco in Spain? And one Ferdinando Paleologus, descended from Byzantine kings but buried in Barbados? Even north of Seattle, where I grew up, the Strait of Juan de Fuca got its name from a sailor who was born Apostolos Valerianos—a Greek. Greeks are everywhere. And so is the Greek language, which was the language of commerce at the time of Christ, when the Mediterranean seemed the globe's most essential sea. One source tells me that Greek words comprise twelve per cent of the English language—especially in the vocabularies of science, medicine, and literary criticism. Aristotle refers to the *Greikoí*, a people of Epirus, and this name may have come to the Romans as Graeci, which was eventually applied to Hellenes and Romaioi and other peoples united by language, geography, and for most, Orthodox Christianity.

Of course there is also that other "Greece"—the classical world we learn about in school and know in part from fragments in museums, from Homer, whoever he was, from Herodotus and Thucydides and the phenomenal drama of the fifth century BCE. The vestiges of that "Golden Age" and so many others are on show all over Greece (not to mention southern Italy and Asia Minor), and even decorate the new Athens Metro. The modern nation, younger than the United States, identifies with this ancient world, sometimes ironically, and its language and geography are the strongest reasons for doing so.

While in Greece in 1997 I noticed a newspaper cartoon by Kostas Mitropoulos. In it a dazed cow emerged from a cave, above which hung a sign: LABYRINTH OF REAL ESTATE TAXES. In her mouth the cow held a man dressed in the traditional *fustanélla* or kilt. This figure may have represented some hapless bureaucrat, and he was speaking through a cell phone to the Prime Minister: IT'S NOT THE MINOTAUR, MR. SIMITIS! IT'S A MAD COW! It was very revealing about contemporary Greek culture—even the inferiority complex that has haunted modern Greeks in comparison to those of the classical past. From Minotaur to mad cow—what to make of a diminished thing.

Whatever aspects of the classical world remain, they are mixed with a fabulous diversity of cultures—more than even Alexander could have imagined. Greece and "Greece" coexist in ways it would take volumes to sort out, and reading Greece is a project for lifetimes. Any country examined closely could be the subject of endless fascination, but part of the fascination of Greece is its uncanny place in world culture because of what it has represented to the rest of us. The adjectives *democratic, ethnic,* and *political,* which define so much modern experience, are from the ancient Greek. *Autocratic* and *tyrannical* stem from the same language. That ideal democratic moment in fifth-century Athens turns out to have been limited, and to have succumbed finally to corruption and imperial arrogance. No one lives outside history.

DAVID ROESSEL'S AUTHORITATIVE HISTORY, *In Byron's Shadow: Modern Greece in the English and American Imagination,* surveys literary versions of Greece over the past two centuries. This is an entertaining work of scholarship, but also a sobering one for those of us who love Greece and want to write about it. Roessel demonstrates in staggering detail that most writers about Greece have failed abysmally by seeking the ideal rather than relishing the more complex realities of the place. As my prologue suggests, I think Roessel's book possesses an importance beyond the academic field of neo-hellenism or that of postcolonial studies. It is about the imagination, and through its particulars involves us with the problem of any literary endeavor. By discussing myriad ways in which writers have misrepresented Greece, Roessel touches on the epistemological dilemma I have been sketching: what is knowable about other people and why should we bother to try? The fact that a small but important country like Greece provides the focus of his investigation compounds its interest. Greece has so often been used as a mirror, particularly by western democracies, that reading Greece has usually become a process of self-definition.

The nineteenth century's image of Greece derived largely from Byron, who became a martyr with his death at Missolonghi in 1824. Ironically, Byron's relationship to Greece was more complex than his literary output might suggest. He genuinely loved the landscape and language, and seems to have embraced Greeks in more ways than one. The land he first visited in 1809–11 was a rugged outpost of the Ottoman Empire, which had ruled the Greeks since the fifteenth century. Though quite tolerant of other religions, the Ottomans imposed significant restrictions on the lives of Greeks, and for centuries had enacted such terrible policies as the *paidomázoma*, the "harvest of children." By this form of taxation, one male child in five between the ages of ten and twenty could be taken by the Turks and forced to join the Sultan's elite corps, the Janissaries. Though most Greek peasants enjoyed a fair amount of local autonomy, they also received little or nothing in return for heavy taxation. This basic injustice, coupled with the corruption of sultans and pashas and the general European movement toward nationalism in the eighteenth century, had led to rebellion, first in the Peloponnesus in 1770, then among the Suliotes of Epirus in 1803, the latter ending in the famous massacre. Greek national consciousness arose, in other words, at the time of the American and French revolutions, but also with nationalist movements elsewhere in Europe. Often these movements were defined not only by geographical borders but by new ideas of language and lexicography. Greek nationalism came with an intellectual emphasis on the classical origins of the modern tongue.

The problem of any classically educated writer falling in love with Greece was how to reconcile the provincial reality of the place, where there had never been any central authority other than the Orthodox Church, with idealized images of Periclean Athens. The fact that such idealizations of Athens were at least partly fictional did not help, nor did the fact that the Greeks who rose up against the Turks were less a unified people than a network of tribes under local chieftains.

Byron was thirty-six when he died. He had made a mess of his personal life, to say the least, and had become a scandal even as a poet. His affection for Greece and his republican convictions were inextricably combined with a desire to save himself and give his life new meaning beyond poetry, which he had begun to doubt. He was realistic enough to see that Greek independence would not occur without foreign aid, and was a good deal more practical about such things than many give him credit for. At Missolonghi he was killed not only by a fever, but also by doctors who bled him, as various military plans had bled his bank account. He died just as he was beginning to prove himself under difficult conditions, leaving his masterpiece, *Don Juan*, unfinished. Compounding all the ironies of his life, he became a symbol of Greece as a romantic European cause, and may have done more for Greece by dying than he could have accomplished if he lived.

But Roessel amply demonstrates that the image of Byron dying for Greece also compromised Greece in many people's minds, and Byron's poems participated in certain myths and prejudices that subsequent writers would perpetuate. If versions of ancient Greece contributed to democratic nationalist ideals in Europe and America, so the modern Greek revolution was usually viewed as the resurrection of classical Athens. Europeans "had no interest in allowing modern Greeks to be modern Greeks," Roessel writes, and he points out that a modern Greek self-definition would have more to do with Constantinople and Byzantium than with Pericles: ". . . radical philhellenes were not attracted to the Orthodox faith of the Greeks, and Christians in the West considered it a debased form of Christianity in need of instruction."

By contrast, Byron himself had been an accomplished neohellenist:

He translated Romaic (modern Greek) songs and attached an appendix of Romaic authors at the end of *Childe Harold*. The most important of the translations was the "War Song" of Rhigas, which appeared in the first edition of *Childe Harold* and in subsequent editions of Byron's verse. Rhigas was a Greek patriot inspired by the French Revolution; he had even hoped for French aid in setting up a republic in Greece. He established himself in 1796 in Vienna, where he wrote prose and poetry to prepare his countrymen for the future rebellion. In 1797, spurred by French victories in Italy and the French occupation of the Ionian Islands, he left Vienna to ask Napoleon for assistance in Greece. Rhigas was arrested by the Austrians in Trieste and turned over to the Turks. He was executed in Belgrade in 1798.

It's a typically Balkan tale with a typically Greek twist in having the "War Song" transformed into a rallying cry by a Romantic poet writing in English. Roessel quotes the third stanza of Byron's version, which advocates modern rebellion in ancient terms:

> Sparta, Sparta, why in slumbers,
> Lethargic dost thou lie?
> Awake, and join thy numbers
> With Athens, old ally!
> Leonidas recalling,
> That chief of ancient song,
> Who sav'd ye once from falling,
> The terrible! The strong!
> Who made that bold diversion
> In old Thermopylae.

Never mind the obvious irony that a twenty-five-year war with Sparta eventually wrecked Athenian democracy. Roessel finds a subtler one: Rhigas "had modeled his 'War Song' on the French national anthem, *La Marseillaise*. If Byron's translation of Rhigas's poem made an English audience think that the Greeks held the same views about the revival of Greece as readers in London, it was because Rhigas had sought to propagate those ideas in his native land. As Byron himself must have realized, the great majority of Greeks who he met in the Levant would not have known who Leonidas was."

In example after example, Roessel finds philhellenic authors to be deluded romantics, sometimes perpetuating sexist and racist stereotypes (a feminized Greece raped by barbarian Turks), usually sacrificing anything like literary merit in the process. The sheer ghastliness of much of the literature Roessel surveys is one of the few dispiriting aspects of his brilliant book. Greece seems to have turned most writers not into swine but blithering idiots. When he expands his survey to take account of the larger region in his chapter called "Pet Balkan People," Roessel finds the literature equally dismal. After quoting Oscar Wilde's ludicrous "Sonnet on the Massacre of the Bulgarian Christians" Roessel concludes, "The literature of Balkan freedom did not produce a single work that has entered the English or American canon, in large part because it originated as a derivative branch of an already ossified philhellenic language." Rather than seeking accurate expressions of their own, writers were feeding off the corpus of Byron and his imitators.

Roessel follows such misunderstandings through the history of modern Greece from independence to the fall of the Colonels in 1974. He locates the historic moment at which philhellenic concerns became conflated with others by the use of a new adjective, Balkan. He notes the impact of the Cretan Revolt of 1866–69, the Greco-Turkish War of 1897, the Balkan Wars, the Gallipoli campaign, the disaster at Smyrna in 1922, the generation-long struggle between republican Venizelists and Greek royalists, the Metaxas dictatorship, World War II and the Greek Civil War (lasting together most of the decade of the forties), the troubled post-war politics and the Junta of 1967–74. In general he finds permutations of the same set of delusions. Greece attracts the adolescent in us, that portion of our experience devoted more to finding ourselves than to seeing the world outside us. As Ford Madox Ford noted in his 1909 essay, "Little States and Great Nations," the country of Greece

"has been turned into a kind of Yellowstone Park, into a reserve where strange races quarrel futilely in a territory that
appears not to be worth commercial exploitation."

It is precisely the unspoiled and Arcadian aspect of Greece
that, in the twentieth century, provided new shadings of philhellenism. But this Arcadian vision arose in spite of a volatile
modern history. One turning point in Roessel's account is the
Smyrna disaster. Given huge portions of Asia Minor by the
Treaty of Sèvres, the Greeks made a terrible miscalculation,
thinking they could recapture more territory and even Constantinople. This is precisely when Mustafa Kemal, who would
later take the name Atatürk, rose up from the rubble of the
Ottoman Empire and forged a modern Turkish state in part
by opposing Greece. Greeks had plundered Turkish towns,
and now they were repaid by being pushed out of Turkey altogether, a retreat culminating in the ashes of Smyrna. Roessel's fascinating discussion of this event takes its title from
Hemingway's short story, "On the Quai at Smyrna." Among
the more compelling aspects of the chapter is his discussion
of what makes Hemingway's fictionalized reportage of events
better than the lies of John Dos Passos, and how Hemingway
contributed to more realistic ways of writing about Greece.

He also discusses Robert Byron, the extraordinary young
man who was among the first foreigners to recognize the cultural importance of Byzantium. Still another major shift in
Western perceptions of Greece took place because certain modern Greek writers were translated and recognized in broader
literary circles. Constantine Cavafy (1863–1933) was surely
among the most important of these—"discovered" by E. M.
Forster and published in T. S. Eliot's *Criterion*. Cavafy was not
only one of the great cultural synthesizers of modern poetry,
a writer of Yeats's generation without a shred of Yeats's romanticism. He was also a love poet who wrote frankly about
homosexuality. Roessel's book notices the irony in how much
European and American gay life began to focus on Athens as if

Cavafy had lived there, when in fact the city he made central to his poems was Alexandria. Despite this fuzzy geography, certain homosexual writers from William Plomer to James Merrill associated Cavafy with the sexual freedom they found in Athens. They could have liaisons with young Greek men who would eventually marry (Greek women being relatively inaccessible outside marriage in those days), and so there was never a risk of attachment or commitment. Greece became associated with sexual freedom at first among gays, but eventually among foreign heterosexuals who were not limited by Greek family ties and conservative social mores. Especially in the sixties and later, Greece became the sexual playground of tourists—certainly more often than it was for the Greeks.

Another modern Greek poet who contributed to a literary reinvention of the culture was George Seferis (1900–1971). Seferis extended the use of demotic Greek in poetry, and expressed themes of exile and historical fragmentation in more personal ways, making his poems attractive to Greek readers as well as foreigners. Having lost his childhood home at Smyrna, Seferis was obsessed by questions of identity; his anxieties were those of many modern Greeks, whether or not they were intellectuals. Significantly for Roessel's history, the "moment" of Seferis coincided with that of Henry Miller and Lawrence Durrell. Miller's *The Colossus of Maroussi* (1941), based upon a relatively slight acquaintance with Greece, is one of the most vivid books ever written on the subject. Though the book is a bit nutty in some of its assertions, Miller's heart is in the right place. Seferis noted that Miller came to Greece without the preconceptions of a classical education, and the enthusiastic American was uniquely able to cherish the country right under his nose. Led to Greece in 1939 by his friend Durrell, Miller met some of the country's leading artists, including Seferis and Nikos Ghika, as well as the scholar George Katsimbalis, and he met those figures as they were involved in a new expression of demotic Greek culture.

Without Miller's book, and several of those by Durrell, other strong accounts of Greece would be unthinkable. Among these, Roessel discusses Patrick Leigh Fermor's *Mani* (1958), Kevin Andrews's *The Flight of Ikaros* (1959), John Fowles' *The Magus* (1965), and Don DeLillo's *The Names* (1982). Andrews, as Roessel correctly observes, was one of the few writers to move beyond self-discovery in Greece and involve himself with the political realities of the Civil War and after. I think Roessel missteps slightly in suggesting that Leigh Fermor avoids discussing the Civil War in preference to a pastoral vision of Greece, but the subject comes up more often in *Roumeli* (1966) than in *Mani*.

This new philhellenism, or New Byronism as Seferis called it, is new chiefly in one respect. Instead of searching for an ideal Greece, the best of these writers *listened* to the Greeks themselves. Instead of just reading Greece, they were hearing the Greek people, and hearing some of their contradictions, their ferocious generosity, their loves and prejudices—their *reality*. This is Roessel's best point, and he makes it almost in passing. It's as if the Greeks were being heard for the first time since Byron tried to hear them in 1824.

Roessel does not leave it there, of course. He points out that Greece was still only partly heard by these writers. Usually it was the pastoral Greece, sharing some of Seferis's nostalgia for lost cultural wholeness. Younger Greek writers—those now in their fifties—have sometimes rejected that nostalgia in favor of a more ironic and urban view. And younger foreigners like Rachel Hadas have cast a cold eye on the cultural limitations of Greece, such as its pervasive sexism. Daughter of a famous classicist, Hadas has had a long relationship with the country in its various guises. Roessel quotes from her poem "Last Trip to Greece" to good effect:

> I had the labels ready with their essence:
> Add water, serve. Light, language, beauty, sea,
> body, etcetera, etcetera. Time.

In honesty I had to change the tune:
quesiness, boredom, and misogyny.

Such ironic reappraisals are partly due to the excesses of writers like Henry Miller, partly to an awareness of how easy it is
to sentimentalize Greece, partly to the cultural damage done
by the dictatorship of the Junta. It was during the Junta that
Mary Lee Settle left the island of Kos for Bodrum in Turkey
(see her *Turkish Reflections: A Biography of a Place*, 1991), and
others followed suit. In the 1980s tourism began to leave the
Greeks feeling jaded while tourism in Turkey increased. Many
Greeks have been worried about this, even with their ambiv-
alence concerning globalization. Being loved can damage a
country as much as being neglected.

Roessel's book stops there, leaving his generation (which
is also mine) with the problem he has so carefully elucidated:
"With Missolonghi so near, it was still almost impossible to
think sanely about Greece." *In Byron's Shadow* is not only an
essential contribution to the study of Greece, but a lively and
compelling story of reading, writing, the imagination, and
what these things have to do with historical reality. The only
quibbles I can make are these: I wish he had quoted more from
the marvelous Edward Lear, who wrote about Crete and main-
land Greece with delightful inventiveness and few illusions; I
wish he had said more about Patrick Leigh Fermor's matchless
prose, which is as gorgeous as any modern writer's; and I wish
he had given a fuller discussion of Kevin Andrews's *Flight of
Ikaros*, certainly one of the most impassioned and realistic evocations of Greece in English.

ONE PHILHELLENE WHOM ROESSEL discusses very well is his
former professor, Edmund Keeley, whose experience of Greece
dates back to his childhood in the thirties. Through his translations, his critical prose, and his fiction, Keeley has done more
for the study of modern Greece than almost any other figure.

I would like to end this essay by mentioning Keeley's latest novel, *Some Wine for Remembrance*. I read the book right after finishing Roessel's study, and was struck again by how well Keeley has *listened* to Greeks, how well he catches their speech, how fully he loves Greek people and their culture. This novel details a German atrocity, the retaliatory massacre of civilians in a village near Thessaloniki during World War II—the very scandal involving Austria's Kurt Waldheim that we were reading about a few years ago.

Fittingly, Keeley structures his story as a sort of *Rashomon* or *Citizen Kane*, a cluster of versions collected by an American journalist with some personal investment in finding the truth. As such, the novel deals with the elusiveness of truth, the difficulty of knowing, even the problem of translation as it pertains to both history and literature. Two Greek characters are "heard" in this novel, and heard very beautifully. One of these loved an Austrian soldier, and it is equally significant that Keeley "hears" figures on the other side. This sympathetic but unsentimental act of listening to other people strikes me as one of the finest things any writer can do. Keeley's novel is rare in its compassion and accuracy. Like all of the best writing about Greece, it teaches us about much more than Greece, and it is also a good, gripping story. By pairing these two new books, Roessel's history and Keeley's novel, I mean honor to them both.

Walking into the Heart of Greece

KEVIN ANDREWS

As a boy in 1940s Greece, my friend Costas had a pistol shoved in his face by a communist *andártis* (guerilla fighter) screaming that he wanted to requisition the family mule. Knowing what the animal meant to his family's survival in desperate times, Costas refused. He might have been shot then and there if the *andártis* had not been restrained by more compassionate comrades. Many years later, attending his nephew's wedding in Athens, Costas was stunned to recognize the best man. It was the very fellow who had once nearly killed him over a mule.

Such stories are common in Greece, where the merciless occupation by Germans and Italians during Word War II, long-standing conflict between left and right, and foreign meddling during the civil war and the Junta years left many Greeks living cheek by jowl with enemies they could never forgive.

It was into this dangerous countryside that the writer Kevin Andrews walked during the civil war (roughly 1945–49). The book he later produced from these travels remains not only one of the greatest we have about post-war Greece—a village culture that has almost vanished behind the new economy and new economic woes—but also one of the most moving accounts I have ever read of people caught up in political turmoil. It is arguably richer, for example, than George Orwell's *Homage to Catalonia* because Andrews spent more time getting to know the people he wrote about. *The Flight of Ikaros* was first published in 1959 and last reprinted by Penguin in 1984. For too many years this rare account has languished out of print, perhaps due to its author's untimely death by drowning in 1989. Let us hope the new edition will see it through to renewed attention and long life.

Born half English, half American in China in 1924, Andrews was well educated but incapable of leading a conventional life. He saw combat with the 10th Mountain Division in Italy, graduated Harvard in 1947, and set out to study archeology in Greece. A Fulbright Fellowship for which he was the only applicant allowed him to spend years in country, working on his study, *Castles of the Morea* (1953). Research was largely conducted on foot, the author entering rugged villages of the Peloponnesus in perilous times, when mountains hid bands of *andártes* and towns were full of soldiers and suspicious police.

Though *The Flight of Ikaros* occasionally sketches the larger political picture, the sources of the civil war and effects of America's Marshall Plan, Andrews' sympathies lie consistently with the ordinary—I should say extraordinary—people he encounters. His politics were clearly of the left, and in 1975 he would renounce his American citizenship in fury over our support of the absurd and incompetent Junta, yet many of the villagers he first befriended were rightists, royalists or worse—like Kostandí, a hardened killer living in the ruins of the Byzantine city, Mistras, exuberantly generous with his foreign friend but deeply compromised by his past. Kostandí's wife trusts Andrews enough to tell him the gripping story of the battle for the hilltop castle, where *andártes* charged outnumbered soldiers, and also the tale of a crazy feud between the killer and his brother: "I said, 'Kotso, did you kill him?' because I saw his hands, his whole body covered with blood. But he only laughed. 'Him? No, he got away through the upper gate . . . Why do you look at me like that? Before dawn this morning I killed sixteen men . . . Now give me my baby and take my clothes and wash them.'"

It is, to use a phrase so often associated with Greece, a scene straight out of Homer. Andrews expertly captures the speech and manners of villagers, and they in turn are intrigued by the foreigner dressed in rags who sleeps in their homes or under the stars. He had a perfect ear for the conversation, the rumors, the paranoia, as well as the generosity of rural Greeks. Roger Jinkinson's biography, *American Ikaros*, suggests that in person Andrews was a difficult man lacking empathy for others. You would never guess it from his affectionate portraits here. His tough embrace and intimate dramas develop a near-mythic intensity.

Diagnosed with epilepsy, Andrews spends time in a Greek hospital, where he meets Nikiphóros, a savagely funny young man whose frustrated vitality could break any reader's heart. Later, he becomes *koumbáros*, or godfather, to the child of a royalist shepherd, Andoni, a man who finds a visit to Athens utterly baffling:

> He looked across the shabby, humble, sprawling little town to the blurred outlines of the mountains he knew better, and then back up at the columns of the Parthenon, and said, "Who made these things, Koumbáre?"
>
> "People who lived here thousands of years ago."
>
> And he said, "Things like this are from God."

Distracted by his study of castles, his climb on Mt. Olympus, and encounters with other acutely rendered characters, Andrews takes a long time getting back to his godson's family. When he finally does, it is to acknowledge that he will soon return to America and does not know whether he will see them again. "I sat on, trying to memorize the position of all the objects in the room—they weren't many. And then something inside me cracked, and I turned away quickly. Andoni leaped up and clasped my head in his arm." The full but understated emotion of this scene is typical of Andrews at his best.

America did not work out. Andrews eventually married a daughter of the poet E. E. Cummings and returned to Greece with his family. The couple separated during the Junta years, she taking their children abroad while Andrews stubbornly stayed on. Among his books, most of which remain nearly impossible to find, are studies of Athens, two longer poems, and a volume called *Greece in the Dark: 1967–1974*, perhaps the best account in English of resistance to the Colonels' regime. It stirringly recreates the major protest marches in which Andrews took part, as well as the funeral of Greece's first Nobel Prize-winning poet, George Seferis. Fiercely opposed to authority, Andrews never assumed any importance for himself, and as a result I trust his narrative voice completely. "Does anything impoverish like caution?" he writes, and most of us will feel a twinge of regret about our more conventional paths, perhaps combined with relief at having avoided some of his mistakes.

One day in 1989 he set out to swim the rough waters off Kythera. He was heading for Avgó (Egg), a little islet said to be Aphrodite's birthplace. Did he have a seizure or just exhaust himself? No one knows. His body was recovered the next day.

Few would call Andrews' life a success. He was too much a loner, too contrary. But he left behind at least one indisputably great book, evocative and painful, restrained and full of compassionate feeling. The Greece remembered here is in many ways disappearing or far removed from what most tourists see in our time. But if you feel you don't really need another book about Greece, Andrews will convince you otherwise. His characters are people you need to encounter in all their flinty reality, their contradiction, their resistance.

So He'll Go
No More A-Roving

PATRICK LEIGH FERMOR

TOWARD THE END of his life, the great writer, war hero, and traveler Sir Patrick Leigh Fermor, who died at age 96, grew deaf and suffered from poor eyesight, sometimes wearing a rakish eye patch to correct his vision. But when I saw him last September he was still volubly alert, his memory undimmed as he retold stories of World War II. His hair was thick, hardly grayed, and his hands resting on the tablecloth resembled knots of wood. We were seated outside for lunch beneath the Byzantine-styled arches of his villa in southern Greece. Ilex trees cast shadows on the stone walls, and waves washed the rocky beach nearby.

It was good to be back.

Thirty years ago, my first wife and I had lived in a tiny stone hut next door to this magnificent house on a bay called Kalamitsi, land once considered sacred to the Nereids, sea nymphs of Greek myth. A young would-be writer, I was given the great gift of friendship by Paddy and his wife, Joan. They meant as much to me as models of gracious living as anyone I have ever known. Joan (tall, angular, quiet, unfailingly wise) died in 2003, and Paddy soldiered on in her absence, buoyed by friends and his own unkillable enthusiasm for life.

In September, Paddy talked of the British retreat from northern Greece nearly seventy years earlier, how he and several companions in a Special Operations Executive unit found themselves making a mad dash south with a suitcase of money meant to shore up the Greek war effort. They bought a fishing boat, but it was shot out from under them by dive-bombing Stukas, "sending the suitcase and all that money straight to Davy Jones"—and several British commandos, Paddy among them, into the Aegean to swim for their lives. Following more trials, they made it to Crete in time for another battle and another retreat.

Paddy would return to the island by parachute in 1942 to live in the caves and mountains among shepherds and guerrilla fighters. He is best known for having kidnapped the German commander of the Cretan occupation in 1944—a story often related with romantic dash and brio and even made into a movie. Dirk Bogarde portrayed Paddy onscreen in *Ill Met by Moonlight* (1957). Yet Paddy himself avoided starring roles. The movie was based on a fellow officer W. Stanley Moss's book on the raid, and Paddy preferred translating a Greek account by George Psychoundakis, *The Cretan Runner* (1955), to writing his own.

Never inclined to introspection, Paddy was endlessly curious about the world, and that curiosity distinguished his life and writing from our confessional age. He insisted that the reference library be near the dining-room table for consultation during mealtime arguments. Once, as he recounted in his lecture, "The Aftermath of Travel," he started researching "the distribution of crocodiles on the Upper Volta River, where I had never been or ever wanted to go. I took down the right volume of the Encyclopedia, but must have opened it at the wrong page, for three weeks later I had read the complete works of Voltaire, but I still knew nothing about the distribution of those crocodiles."

WHAT MADE PADDY FAMOUS as a writer—or as famous as a writer's writer can be—was his narrative of walking from Holland to Constantinople in the early 1930s. The writing was spurred by the unexpected recovery of diaries that he had assumed were lost forever, and what resulted was a pair of masterpieces, *A Time of Gifts* (1977) and *Between the Woods and the Water* (1986). A third volume completing the journey is still awaited. The glacial pace of Paddy's writing frustrated many readers, but his weaving and unweaving of sentences resulted in some of the richest English prose we have. Here he is in Vienna with a young Frisian Islander who learned his English from reading Shakespeare:

> Our way back took us along the Graben and the Kärntnerstrasse. About lamplighting time, I had noticed a small, drifting population of decorative girls who shot unmistakable glances of invitation at passersby. Konrad shook his head. "You must beware, dear young," he said in a solemn voice. "These are wenches and they are always seeking only pelf. They are wanton, and it is their wont."

The particular exuberance of his prose came from endless revision, where he added layer upon layer of detail as his mind leapt nimbly across cultures and centuries. He wrote to me in 1985 about the second volume: "I have just put the mss on the Oitylo-Athens bus where it is to be met by the typist, who will get to work on it at once: now for pruning, revision, scissors and paste, the moment I get it back." His manuscripts were fringed with emendations, often covered with fanciful scrawls and illustrations.

I have a copy of one of them, "Notes on the Hellespont," sent to me after he had celebrated his seventieth birthday by swimming that legendary strait. The typescript is covered not only with marginal arrows and alterations but also with seagulls, clouds, and waves drawn with his fountain pen. "I was swimming sidestroke, and began to notice a strange fluctuating and hissing noise under my submerged left ear; it was very eerie, like an echo in a vast dark room below, and I thought it must have been the grinding of pebbles and silt at the bottom of the sea."

It was after his long walk to Constantinople that Paddy gained intimate knowledge of Greece. On the plains of Thessaly, he participated in a cavalry charge during one of that country's frequent political upheavals, and in Athens he fell in love with a Romanian princess. He lived with her in a windmill in the Peloponnese and then on her rambling estate in Moldova. But when war came in 1939, he returned home and enlisted in the Irish Guards.

After the war—during which he met Joan in Cairo—there were more peregrinations around the Mediterranean and the Caribbean, the last of these resulting in *The Traveller's Tree: A Journey Through the Caribbean Islands* (1950) and his only novel, *The Violins of Saint-Jacques* (1953).

He and Joan knew they could never settle in Crete, where his wartime actions and subsequent friendships would result in an endless string of feasts and raki-drinking sprees that would have killed him in a Byronic flash. Instead their travels in Greece led them into the isolated middle peninsula of the southern Peloponnese: the Mani, walled off from the rest of Greece by the Taygetus Mountains. There they constructed one of the world's most inspired houses—not ostentatious in size but perfectly integrated into the landscape and culture of the region. Its walled garden, cypress and olive groves, and the adjacent sea made the house feel open to the world, with terraces for intimate meals and spaces of quietude filled only by birdsong.

They lived in tents while the house was built. "We were given the raw-material free—grey, fawn, russet and apricot-coloured limestone—which we hacked, prized and blew out of the side of the Taygetus and roughly dressed with claw-chisels," he wrote in "The Aftermath of Travel." Our lunch last September was eaten near "a heavy stone lintel seven feet long, salvaged from a demolition in Tripoli," as Paddy recounted. "Roping it to a ladder, twelve of us sweated and swore and stumbled under it for a quarter of a mile down the steep tiers of the olive-groves and through a flock of sheep. The simple-hearted shepherd asked us what we were going to do with it and our godbrother answered through clenched teeth: 'We're going to chuck it in the sea, to see if it floats!'"

Until the house was completed, Paddy was always writing in other people's homes. He wrote the greatest of his books about Greece, *Mani: Travels in the Southern Peloponnese* (1958), at the home of the painter Nikos Ghika on the island of Hydra. The next volume, *Roumeli: Travels in Northern Greece*, was drafted in France, Italy, and England but finally finished at Kalamitsi in 1966. And I think it was the glorious dwelling with its large studio, its sea-pebbled terrace and shady isolation that made his later masterpieces possible.

But it also provided a temptation to countless visitors from all over the world. Paddy and the villa became a coveted destination for endless travelers. I met the likes of Stephen Spender, Bruce Chatwin, the publisher John Murray, and the historian Steven Runciman passing by my hut, where I lived a lotus-eating life by the sea without electricity or running water. If I share some guilt for distracting Paddy from writing over the years, my gratitude overcomes it.

Paddy and Joan lent me books, fed me, regaled me with stories, introduced me to their friends, and never once required proof that I was a personage of any stature. They were the most generous human beings I have ever known, and my own "time of gifts" began in their company. I walked with Paddy in the hills, swam with him in the sea, and kept him apprised of my own crooked path in life. "I write in sackcloth and ashes," he would joke when his letters were delayed, and would proceed to supply me with drafts of his intoxicating verbal vintage.

Paddy was not a travel writer—the term is an idiotic reduction for the purposes of marketing. He was a poet, a fantastic re-creator of experience, a maker of paradisiacal sentences that leave me hungry for life. Chatwin chided him for his verbal embroidery, but what a rare thing it is to find the baroque in our time, and Paddy was just as capable of the simple observation—turning on a tap in an overheated Greek village and seeing nothing but a lonely cockroach crawl out of it, or hearing the conversation of Greeks muffled by a bedroom wall, as he noted in *Mani*: "The soft murmur of the town was suddenly drowned by the furious jay-like voices of two women below my window, arguing across a narrow lane about something I couldn't catch. It didn't matter. The point was the inventive richness of the language, the splendour of the vocabulary, the unstaunchable flow of imagination and invective. . . . I can actually see the words spin from their mouths like long balloons in comic strips."

He had the good luck, or bad, depending on your point of view, to become a legend in his own lifetime. He saw the remote part of Greece he had chosen for his home commercialized and was himself the subject of innumerable tours by people far less likely to sweat for their adventures. None of this bothered him, as far as I could see. Now that he is dead, friends exclaim to me: "What a life!" Indeed, and what books he made of it—their breadth and style worthy shadows of the man himself.

2011

The News from Everywhere

BRUCE CHATWIN

BRUCE CHATWIN WAS BORN as a writer at age thirty-four in
Argentina. He had proved himself as a magazine journalist,
but in 1974 he was on the trail of a story, or a set of braided
stories, that would become his first book: *In Patagonia*, a cult
classic of the travel genre. You can see the excitement he felt
in his letters: "Buenos Aires is utterly bizarre a combination of
Paris and Madrid shorn of historical depth, with hallucinat-
ing avenidas flanked with lime trees, where not even the hum-
blest housewife need forgo the architectural aspirations of
Marie Antoinette." Or a month later, in January 1975: "I have
been caught in the lost beast fervour and 2 days ago scaled an
appalling cliff to the bed of an ancient lake . . . and there discovered to my inexpressible delight a collection of fragments
of the carapace of the glyptodon. The glyptodon has if anything replaced the mylodon in my affections—there are about
6 whole ones in the Museum of La Plata—an enormous arma-
dillo up to 9–10 feet long, each scale of its armour looking like
a Japanese chrysanthemum."

It's all there: the headlong pace, the nimble precision with a dash of snobbery, the obsession with the minutiae of far places, the charm of a man who could turn on a dime to jaw-dropping lectures on scenes you'd never dreamed of. It's pure Chatwin.

THE LEGENDARY TRAVELER'S BOOKS are set not only at the tip of South America but also in Dahomey (now Benin), the Welsh border country, Australia, and communist Czechoslovakia. His death in 1989 sent a global village of readers into shocked mourning. He had become our Byronic hero, not only for his tersely stylish prose and dashing looks but also for the apparent freedom with which he lived. (I knew Chatwin slightly, and a handful of his postcards to me appear in *Under the Sun*, a selection of his letters, with much more substantial correspondence to others.) When we learned that the Chatwin of the books was not quite the man himself—and that the man himself was more complicated than we realized, not always admirable, even prone to callousness and deception, that he had led a double life as a gay sexual tourist while creating his literary legend—some readers felt betrayed. At times the critical backlash was scathing in its denunciation. But reading his letters, edited by his widow and by his expert biographer, Nicholas Shakespeare, adds complicated shadings to our portrait. We can see Chatwin developing from a narcissistic know-it-all, who used his wife as a base of domesticity while pursuing a wholly separate sexual identity, to a kind of pilgrim—a husband, friend, and exacting writer of great originality and ambition.

Charles Bruce Chatwin was born in Sheffield, England, in 1940, the son of a lawyer who had been called to war by the Naval Reserves. The letters reveal three pertinent elements to his childhood: the trauma of wartime England, where he was often on the move with his mother; his early interest in books about travel; and a precocious fascination with things—collecting and learning the value of objects. By age seventeen he was already dealing in antique furniture, writing his parents from school: "Aunt Cicely and Uncle Philip sent 10/- [shillings] for a Wallace Collection catalogue."

He was an indifferent student. It was decided that a job at Sotheby's would suit him better than university. At the auction house he rose rapidly from "numbering porter in the Works of Art Department" to director of "Antiquities and Impressionists and Modern Art." He met Elizabeth Chanler, an American working for the firm, and they were married in her family's chapel in upstate New York in 1965. By age twenty-six he was a partner in the firm but already sick of the art world, suffering a case of psychosomatic blindness and writing to a friend: "Never sit out your life at a desk."

Chatwin early developed his mania for travel—which his wife shared, though he often traveled alone or with male friends. He was a collector of distant destinations, writing at fourteen from Sweden, eighteen from Beirut and Sardinia, at twenty from Greece, at twenty-one from Egypt. One of the first lengthy letters found in *Under the Sun* is to his mother from Afghanistan, a country he loved deeply: "To the bazaar in a curricle, jingling with bells and hung with red pom-poms. You sit back to back, the form of these vehicles hasn't changed since Alexander used one to cross from here to India." He was twenty-three years old. Seventeen years later he would write "A Lament for Afghanistan," after the Russian invasion, as a preface to his favorite travel book, Robert Byron's *The Road to Oxiana*: "Where now is the Hakim of Kande? We stayed in his summerhouse under a scree of shining schist and watched the creamy clouds coming over the mountains." Distance in time and the intervening war have only made the piece more heartbreaking.

It's not just that Chatwin saw a lot of places before they were destroyed by tourism or conflict. It's more that his eye for art objects had become an eye for human eccentricities, often hauntingly expressed. *In Patagonia* (1977) begins in his grandmother's dining room with a cabinet containing among its treasures a dried piece of mylodon skin sent by a cousin, "Charley Milward the Sailor." From that odd inspiration the writer quests outward into a world of strange beauty and marginal lives. "All the stories are chosen," he wrote to an American friend, "with the purpose of illustrating some particular aspect of wandering and/or exile: i.e., what happens when you get stuck. The whole should be an illustration of the Myth of Cain and Abel."

The book arrived during a vogue for travel writing and sold well. Yet, contrary to the hype he sometimes encouraged, Chatwin was never really a travel writer. He "was a storyteller first," Shakespeare noted in his 1999 biography, "but not until the last third of his life did he write the stories down." Chatwin told an Australian journalist: "The borderline between fiction and non-fiction is to my mind extremely arbitrary." He invented needed details and used people as well as objects in his stories—but this hardly distinguishes him from a host of successful writers.

In Patagonia was a phantasmagoria of mythology, history, and the author's restless personality. His next book, *The Viceroy of Ouidah* (1980), was intended to do the same for the slave trade in Africa, but a coup in which Chatwin was roughed up by Benin soldiers disrupted his research, and he "went on to write a work of the imagination." Cold and often perfunctory, it is not a beguiling story. Chatwin's two best books, *On the Black Hill* (1982) and *Utz* (1988), concern people whose lives are painfully circumscribed but, like Chatwin's own, fraught with sexual secrets and a tension between freedom and responsibility.

On the Black Hill tells the story of identical twins, Lewis and Benjamin Jones. Lewis is a frustrated heterosexual, his brother perhaps a closeted gay man, but they share the same bed in a farm called The Vision. Chatwin wrote that this novel was an experiment in "circular time," and it's the way his prose particularizes time's passage, the efficient sweep of the narrative over several thwarted households, that makes it so satisfying. It is full of eccentricity and the odd beauty of people. When the twins are taken up in an airplane for the first time as an 80th birthday present, Lewis reacts in revealing ways. He had always wanted to fly, "and suddenly he felt—even if the engine failed, even if the plane took a nosedive and their souls flew up to Heaven—that all the frustrations of his cramped and frugal life now counted for nothing, because, for ten magnificent minutes, he had done what he wanted to do."

On the Black Hill was followed by Chatwin's big seller: *The Songlines* (1987). Most of us read it as nonfiction—my American edition offers no other label—but the letters make it clear that the author thought of the book as an experiment: "It is, I suppose, a novel: though of a very strange kind." Building on an Aboriginal tradition of "mapping" the land through chant, *The Songlines* is a story of ideas, but when taken as anthropology about nomadism it has infuriated more knowledgeable readers. Chatwin was eager to build on earlier failure—an abandoned early book called *The Nomadic Alternative*—with more recent discoveries by scientists. But Chatwin had far less access to Australian Aborigines than he claimed, and his theory of the benign origins of humanity is sentimental at best.

Still, this jumble-box of arcana intrigues me, and his heroic effort to complete the book while suffering the first symptoms of AIDS is one of the most compelling aspects of the letters. His "vision of the Songlines stretching across the continents and ages" has a wildly attractive quality, like the visionary poems of William Blake. "If this were so; if the desert were 'home'; if our instincts were forged in the desert; to survive the rigors of the desert—then it is easier to understand why greener pastures pall on us; why possessions exhaust us."

If Chatwin, in the words of Nicholas Shakespeare, "traveled as much to leave one self behind as to find another," his final illness settled him. He visited Mt. Athos and declared himself a convert to Greek Orthodoxy. "The search for nomads is a quest for God," he wrote in a notebook. In a brief remission from his disease, he produced the slender, jewel-like *Utz*, a novella about a collector of Meissen porcelain in Prague. The story returned him to original obsessions, but with greater wisdom. There is again a narrator who reconstructs the tale from fragmentary evidence: "Things, I reflected, are tougher than people. Things are the changeless mirror in which we watch ourselves disintegrate."

Chatwin's own disintegration, including delusional shopping sprees from his wheelchair that seemed to recap his life in frenetic miniature, is recounted by his editors, but we can still see growth in him through his final letters: "I have envied and grasped at possessions but they are very bad for me." He had found his real vocation as a writer. Death caught him in the midst of plans for a new novel, as well as a book on healing and a collection of tales.

Chatwin had written much of *The Songlines* in a Greek hotel near the villa of the legendary writer Patrick Leigh Fermor. In 1997, Leigh Fermor took me into the mountains to show me the tiny Byzantine church where he and Elizabeth Chatwin had buried her husband's ashes under an olive tree. I cannot imagine a more fitting grave for this strange, magnificent writer—anonymous, with a view for miles across the sea.

Exiles,
Eccentrics,
Immigrants

Man of Action,
Man of Letters

JOSEPH CONRAD

He knew the magic monotony of existence
between sky and water . . .

   —*LORD JIM*

We can never cease to be ourselves.

   —*THE SECRET AGENT*

I MISS LETTERS, POSTCARDS, AEROGRAMMES—typed or hand-written, arriving with kaleidoscopic stamps, inked with dates and places of origin. They took time and gave weight to words. Often they went out like shared pages from private notebooks, collaborations with the friends and strangers to whom they were sent. Now when real letters arrive I can hardly believe in their existence. Caught from the neck up in the Internet, I have slowly learned that a civil voice still has to be fashioned with patience and calm I do not always possess. It's useful to be reminded that urban and even suburban English dwellers of the early twentieth century could rely on at least two postal deliveries per day—five in central London. Perhaps the

Internet is only a symptom of our convoluted and overpopulated world.

These are customary grumblings from a reviewer of literary letters, laments that do us little good. *The Selected Letters of Joseph Conrad* compels reading and re-reading not because of postal technology, but because the man who inhabits these pages is so remarkable. Laurence Davies' marvelous introduction avers that "Conrad's letters registered warm affection, rage, frustration, recklessness, spiritual prostration, frenzied glee, and occasional malice." I find Conrad's character utterly companionable even in its darker moods. A man of action who spent twenty years at sea and had seen revolutionary politics first hand, he had a scientist's ability to observe both people and the natural world, and was profoundly skeptical of political systems. He loved and wrote in English, which he had only begun to learn as a sailor at age nineteen—neither his native Polish nor his acquired French could satisfy his ambitions or his psychological needs. He maintained complicated literary friendships with some of the major writers of his day, including Henry James, H. G. Wells, Stephen Crane, Ford Madox Ford, and André Gide. During a literary career that began in his late thirties, he mastered not only the novel but also the novella and memoir, and took an interest in stage and film adaptations of his work. His oeuvre, which influenced writers from T. S. Eliot to Gabriel García Márquez as well as filmmakers like Francis Ford Coppola and Werner Herzog, offers disillusioned visions of human relations, motives, and conduct. He was incapable of sentimentality, having beheld the world too clearly. He never fully quit the sea, and helped patrol the coast in the defense of his adopted country during World War I. A man of action as well as a man of letters, he was also a loving friend, a reserved but devoted father and husband. Often crippled by gout and depression, he could be funny, even snappishly satirical, about nearly anything. The letters give us access to the complexity and stature of this magnificent figure. They make me want to re-read Conrad and keep him close.

He was, you might say, groomed for a double life, from the aristocratic reserve of his mother, who died when Conrad was seven, to the romantic élan and revolutionary zeal of his father, a poet and translator of Shakespeare who got himself embroiled in anti-Russian politics. Born Józef Teodor Konrad Korzeniowski in 1857, Conrad was only three years old when his father was arrested for conspiracy; and the following year the child accompanied his parents into exile in Russia. At age ten the motherless boy was taken to Odessa, where he had his first glimpse of the sea. When he was only eleven, living back in Cracow, Conrad saw his father, Apollo, die of tuberculosis. The thronged funeral procession was a major display of Polish nationalism. Conrad would eventually have his own experiences with gunrunners and revolutionaries (his life threatened by both man and nature), but his lifelong fatalism and dislike of all things Russian began in childhood. Writing in 1900 to his close friend Edward Garnett, an author and the husband of Constance Garnett, the well-known translator of Russian literature, Conrad recalled his father in tender terms:

> A man of great sensibilities; of exalted and dreamy temperament; with a terrible gift of irony and of gloomy disposition; withal of strong religious feeling degenerating after the loss of his wife into mysticism touched with despair. His aspect was distinguished; his conversation very fascinating; his face in repose sombre, lighted all over when he smiled. I remember him well. For the last two years of his life I lived alone with him—but why go on?

By the time he wrote these words Conrad was an "established" author, with some of his most famous work, including *Heart of Darkness*, behind him and *Lord Jim* in the pipeline. He was married, living with his wife and a young son, Borys, in the English countryside. Aware that some Poles considered him a traitor for writing in English, and that the English literary establishment (unlike men he had known at sea) still looked on him as an outsider or interloper with a strange grasp of the Queen's language, Conrad struggled to make a place for himself in the world of letters. Though he had always enjoyed the support of his Polish relatives, he was very much a self-made man, having gone to sea and worked his way from mate to captain—on French ships until he turned twenty-one, then in the English merchant navy, learning the new language as an adult. He had made and lost money, had once attempted suicide over debts and a love affair, and had sailed the globe. He had first read Shakepseare and Dickens in Polish translations, some by his father, and had imbibed French literature in his youth, but when he came to England and English he felt he had found his true home, even if it did not quite rush to welcome him. "Both at sea and on land," he wrote to a Polish historian in 1903, "my point of view is English, from which the conclusion should not be drawn that I have become an Englishman. That is not the case. Homo duplex has in my case more than one meaning. You will understand me. I shall not dwell upon the subject." An English point of view, it would seem, maintained the belief in one's own freedom as man and artist.

He approached his writing as he had once studied good seamanship, with a Flaubertian devotion to craft, but was prone to doubts and fits of temperament that sometimes upset family and friends. He was a rarity, and those close to him knew it. A writer of fierce psychological discernment who had the most unusual range of settings and characters to draw upon for his models, he had simply seen more, experienced more, than most writers ever see or experience. As he wrote to a friend in 1907, "Living with memories is a cruel business. I—who have a double life one of them peopled only by shadows growing more precious as the years pass—know what that is."

Though he hated all things Russian, he is often compared to two famous Russian exiles—Nabokov and Brodsky—for this quality of doubleness. But Brodsky never mastered English as well as Conrad or Nabokov, and Nabokov turned nostalgia into high art while Conrad largely suppressed it. Still, it seems worth noting how modern literature in English has been enriched by such artists of psychic and political exile, champions of the individual imagination over the cant of group thinking.

The Cambridge edition of *The Collected Letters of Joseph Conrad* runs to nine volumes, of which I have seen only a few, so I am grateful for Davies' selection here. The jewels are plentiful, the underlinings in my copy copious. Conrad is the sort of writer who teaches on multiple levels—by his insights and observations and the unintended revelations illuminating his books. Letters written about his Congo experiences in 1890 will fascinate readers of *Heart of Darkness*:

> Everything here is repellent to me. Men and things, but men above all. And I am repellent to them, also. From the manager in Africa who has taken the trouble to tell one and all that I offend him supremely, down to the lowest mechanic, they all have the gift of irritating my nerves—so that I am not as agreeable to them perhaps as I should be. The manager is a common ivory dealer with base instincts who considers himself a merchant although he is only a kind of African shop-keeper.

These words were written in French to his beloved aunt, Marguerite Poradowska, to whom he would later write from London:

> I have absolutely nothing to say to you. I am vegetating. I do not even think—therefore I do not exist (according to Descartes). But another individual (a scientist) has said: "Without phosphorus, no thought." From which it seems that I am still there, but the phosphorus is missing. Yet in that case I would exist without thinking, which (according to Descartes)

is impossible. Good heavens! Could I be a Punch? The Punch of my childhood, you know—his spine broken, his nose on the floor between his feet; his legs flung out stiffly in that attitude of profound despair, so pathetically droll, of dolls tossed in a corner.

There is much to relish in a young writer's trying out his style, but we can also see in Conrad's mixture of tones an unsystematic vision of life—the sort of anti-philosophical creativity exemplified by Shakespeare. "But what is the use of plans?" he wrote later to his aunt. "Destiny is our master!"

Conrad's stoic humor enjoys the anarchic, which is partly why his anarchists in *The Secret Agent* are so grimly funny, and his laughter in other tales, like that of Marlow in "Youth," entertains nostalgia at a distance, educated by that "tussle with the sea." His tones are always mixed: you can hear the cosmic laughter in his grimmest passages and weep at his comedy. Even casual lines reveal his warmth toward individuals, his coldness toward the species in general. During World War I he wrote to a friend enduring the German measles, "I am scandalized by your unpatriotic choice of disease." More often than not, he's the butt of his own jokes. After theorizing about Proust to the translator C. K. Scott Moncrieff he concludes, "This is more or less what I think, or imagine that I think. It is really not half of what I imagine I think." In 1923, a year before his death, we find him reporting on a case of the flu suffered along with his wife: "Jessie came out strong a[s] usual. I remained croaky, groggy tottery, staggery, shuddery shivery, seedy, gouty, sorry wretch that I am."

Anyone wanting to learn about the life of a working writer—the labor, the doubts, the constant misreadings and money worries—will find these letters edifying. At the beginning, with only his father's failures and his own rudderless aspirations to guide him, he was tempted to destroy his early work, writing in 1894 to his aunt,

I have burned nothing. One talks like that, but then one lacks the courage. There are those who talk like that of suicide. And then there is always something lacking, sometimes strength, sometimes perseverance, sometimes courage. The courage to succeed or the courage to recognize one's impotence. What remains always cruel and ineradicable is the fear of finality. One temporizes with Fate, one seeks to deceive desire, one tries to play tricks with one's life. Men are always cowards. They are frightened of the expression 'nevermore'. I think only women have true courage.

But he was lucky to be recognized for his talent by friends who became his advocates and champions. Four months after the letter I have just quoted we find him writing to Edward Garnett:

To be read—as you do me the honour to read me—is an ideal experience—and the experience of an ideal; and as I travel from sentence to sentence of your message I feel my unworthiness more and more. Your appreciation has for me all the subtle and penetrating delight of unexpected good fortune—some fabulously lucky accident like the finding of a gold nugget in a deserted claim, like the gleam of a big diamond in a handful of blue earth.

The same man who so thoroughly doubted himself can be found within a few additional months dispensing sage advice to another writer: "You must remember that true worth is never recognized at once." He follows this with one of his many invaluable aesthetic statements:

Remember that death is not the most pathetic—the most poignant thing—and you must treat events only as illustrative of human sensation—as the outward sign of inward feelings—of live feelings—which alone are truly pathetic and interesting. . . . To accomplish it you will have to cultivate your poetic faculty—you must give yourself up to your emotions (no easy task) you must squeeze out of yourself every sensation, every thought, every image—mercilessly, without reserve and without remorse; you must search the darkest corners of your heart, the most remote recesses of your brain;—you must search them for the image, for the glamour, for the right expression. And you must do it sincerely, at any cost; You must do it so that at the end of your day's work you should feel exhausted, emptied of every sensation and every thought, with a blank mind and an aching heart, with the notion that there is nothing—nothing left in you.

To my anthology of Conradian aesthetics I would add this, from a 1903 letter to H. G. Wells: ". . . for me, writing—*the only possible writing*—is just simply the conversion of nervous force into phrases." No wonder he knew himself to be modern. No wonder his influence upon modernism was so profound. He had written in 1902 to the publisher William Blackwood, "I am *modern*, and I would rather recall Wagner the musician and Rodin the Sculptor who both had to starve a little in their day— and Whistler the painter who made Ruskin the critic foam at the mouth with scorn and indignation. . . . My work shall not be an utter failure because it has the solid basis of a definite intention—first: and next because it is not an endless analysis of affected sentiments but in its essence it is action. . . . nothing but action—action observed, felt and interpreted with an absolute truth to my sensations (which are the basis of art in literature)—action of human beings that will bleed to a prick, and are moving in a visible world." To the Scottish writer Helen Sanderson he wrote, "The apparently irrelevant is often illuminative. You must never be afraid of remote connection; you must let your mind range widely about your subject. . . . You must try to say things fully; but do not imagine that I would lead you into verbosity. It is not more words that I recommend but—alas!—more toil." To his protégé and bibliographer Richard Curle he explained, "Explicitness, my dear fellow, is fatal to the glamour of all artistic work, robbing it of all suggestiveness, destroying all illusion. You seem to believe in literalness and explicitness, in facts and also in expression. Yet nothing is more clear than the utter insignificance of explicit statement and also its power to call attention away from things that matter in the region of art."

He is equally perspicacious about specific writers: "It's Henry James and nothing but Henry James. The delicacy and tenuity of the thing are amazing. It is like a great sheet of plate glass—you don't know it's there until you run against it." Asked to comment on the unending debate over who wrote Shakespeare's plays, he gave what I regard as the final word on the subject:

> The Bacon controversy has never interested me because what does it matter to us who wrote Shakespeare's works? I once knew a kind of hermit (he lived in a wooden hut in a small wood) who affirmed absolutely that Shakespeare's works were written by a supernatural being to whom he gave a name I no longer remember. As he seemed greatly attached to this theory, I told him I wished him well but in the end I was wholly indifferent to the question. Straightaway he told me I was an idiot. Thus ended our relations.

It says a lot that he could not stand the Christianity of Tolstoy and Dostoyevsky, and preferred the skeptical humanity of Chekhov in Constance Garnett's translations. He wrote to Edward Garnett in 1914, *"Dislike* as definition of my attitude to Tols[toy] is but a rough and approximate term. I judge him not—for this reason that his antisensualism is suspect to me. . . . Moreover the base from which he starts—Christianity—is distasteful to me. I am not blind to its services but the absurd oriental fable from which it starts irritates me."

Raised a Catholic, Conrad was utterly unsentimental about the intersections of religious and secular culture. A 1923 letter opens, "I have been a stranger to Santa Claus all my life. You'll understand how the Polish children did not need a Germanic fairy saint to give them the sense of sanctity and joy attached to the day of Nativity in the hearts of Roman Catholics." But he had just as little faith in the general run of mankind. It was not only the influence of world war that caused him to write to his literary agent, J. B. Pinker, in 1919 (thinking how the two of them might be seen by posterity), "If the world were honest and fair-minded, it could be trusted with the whole truth. But it isn't. It will put the worst construction on any given episode and besmirch the real truth established by so many years of your determined belief in me and of my gratitude to you which, believe me my dear friend, has never been obscured for a moment in my heart, no matter what words might have been written on the spur of the moment."

His dim views of political idealism are best expressed in a long letter to Bertrand Russell, who in 1922 had published a book about China: "I have never been able to find in any man's book or any man's talk anything convincing enough to stand up for a moment against my deep-seated sense of fatality governing this man-inhabited world. . . . The only remedy for Chinamen and for the rest of us is the change of hearts, but looking at the history of the last 2000 years there is not much reason to expect that thing, even if man has taken to flying—a great 'uplift', no doubt, but no great change. He doesn't fly like an eagle; he flies like a beetle. And you must have noticed how ugly, ridiculous and fatuous is the flight of a beetle." Conrad's great political novels—*Nostromo, The Secret Agent,* and *Under Western Eyes*—are dramatic dissections of failed ideals. But Conrad was not merely reactionary. His views were as complex and contradictory as Darwin's:

> I don't believe in the oneness of life. I believe in its infinite
> variety. And if you tell me that I am a shallow person thinking
> of forms and not of essence, I will tell you that this is all we

have got to hold on to—that form is the artist's (and the scientist's) province that it is all we can understand (and interpret or represent) and that we can't tell what is behind. As to the Eternity of Art—I don't suppose it is more or less eternal than the earth itself. I can't believe in the eternity of art any more than the eternity of pain or eternity of love (subjects of art, those) whose emotions art (and of all arts music) brings home to our breasts. Art for me *is* an end in itself. Conclusions are not for it.

In addition to art he valued friends and his family—his wife Jessie who protected him from many distractions while suffering her own crippling leg injury, and his two children. Many accounts portray Conrad as a distanced and ineffectual father, but his letters reveal close attention to his children as individuals. When Borys went away to war, his father kept close tabs on him, often reporting to friends about the boy (who saw a lot of action and eventually was both gassed and shellshocked). In 1918, with Borys still at war, the Conrads sent their second son, John, away to school. "He looked happy enough. But for me it was sad to behold the dear little pagan in the Eton jacket and horrible round collar of (I suppose) the most Christian civilization in the world." This passage from a letter to Conrad's close friend, the novelist John Galsworthy, is followed by another loving anecdote:

> Those people are really full of kindness and tact (I can see it plainly) but they have not the slightest conception of what he is. They will understand him presently when he has become like one of themselves. But I shall always remember the original—the only genuine John—as long as I live. Borys too had a particular impression of "The Kid" which he could not define any better than I can mine. And he too will be sorry. As to Jessie they were too close together, she really loved him too much to see him clearly. She'll always be delighted with him.

We took Nellie [Jessie's sister] with us. On the way back she said: "Doesn't John look well!" (He was most gracious to her). Then after a long while she said as if to herself: "Poor John".

In letters like this, the tragic stoicism of Joseph Conrad—his love of mortal particulars more than the general or ideal— arises from a single, undivided heart.

A Mad Master
of Modernism

EZRA POUND

ON JAN. 30, 1933, the American poet Ezra Pound was granted an audience with the leader he most admired, Italy's Benito Mussolini. Il Duce's Roman office, as Pound's latest biographer describes it, was "a vast room forty feet high, sixty feet in length, and as wide as it was high. The space was quite empty from one end to the other except for the desk at which Mussolini worked. . . . He insisted on absolute silence, no sound being allowed in from the piazza outside, and if a fly buzzed he called for it to be swatted."

"Mussolini asked," in biographer A. David Moody's retelling, "what was his aim in writing *The Cantos*, and Pound replied, 'to put my ideas in order'; and Mussolini said, 'What do you want to do that for?'" When the poet turned from this dismissal to economic policy, which had lately become the central obsession of his life, the dictator was unimpressed by Pound's list of eighteen proposals, alighting particularly on his assertion that "in the Fascist state taxes were no longer necessary": "Have to think about THAT," Mussolini said and ended the interview. To the fascist dictator, Pound, by any measure one of the twentieth century's major literary figures, merited hardly more bother than a fly.

For twenty years, Ezra Pound (1885–1972) had been the dominant promoter of literary Modernism. He had co-founded such movements as Imagism and Vorticism, had befriended and helped such literary giants as W. B. Yeats, James Joyce, T. S. Eliot, Robert Frost, Ernest Hemingway, Hilda Doolittle, and Ford Madox Ford, as well as championing countless artists who were less well known. Pound was indispensable to editors on both sides of the Atlantic, saw to it that Eliot and Frost were promoted in the pages of *Poetry* magazine, and arranged for Joyce's family to settle in Paris between the wars—at one point even mailing Joyce a decent pair of shoes. He performed successful surgery on Eliot's poem of nervous collapse, "The Waste Land," removing its fastidiousness and turning it into a masterpiece.

After Pound moved from Paris to Italy in 1923, he and his lover, violinist Olga Rudge, became champions not just of Modernist composers like George Antheil and Igor Stravinsky but also of the then-neglected Vivaldi, whose manuscripts they retrieved and published, arranging concerts in which old and new music vitally coexisted. And during all this exhaustive and exhausting activity, he wrote his own garrulous prose, poetry, and translations—much of it work of penetrating beauty. Yet by the time he met Mussolini, on the very day that Hitler became chancellor of Germany, Pound was on a downward slide toward madness and ruin, unable to see that his infatuation with politics and economics was destroying him both as an artist and as a man.

The Epic Years 1921–1939 is the second volume of a magnificent biography (a third volume will follow) that will surely take its place among the most important studies of any Modernist writer. Mr. Moody, emeritus professor of literature at

York University, never succumbs to amateur psychoanalysis or gossip. "I have refrained from speculation," he writes, "and I have ignored hearsay." Instead, he relates Pound's life with economy, attention to evidence—letters, published writings, documents—and a meticulous close reading of the work.

The first volume was subtitled *The Young Genius 1885–1920* and was all rising energy, a man bringing dynamism to the arts, especially in London before and during World War I. This was the Pound who gruffly diagnosed the "emotional anaemia" of the time, yet could write with such tenderness in "Alba" (1912):

As cool as the pale wet leaves
        of lily-of-the-valley
She lay down beside me in the dawn.

This was the poet who, using the manuscripts of Ernest Fenollosa, movingly invented Chinese poetry for modern English readers and quirkily re-invented the Latin elegy in "Homage to Sextus Propertius" (1919): "Shades of Callimachus, Coan ghosts of Philetas / It is in your grove I would walk, / I who come first from the clear font / Bringing the Grecian orgies into Italy."

The second volume begins with Pound's move to Paris from London in 1921 and carries him up to a trip to the US in the last prewar summer. It is a dispiriting story, Pound channeling his genius into work that seems increasingly wrong-headed, dominated by ideas more than vital experience or new voices. Moody makes a case for Pound's strange musical compositions, such as his 1926 opera, "Le Testament de Villon," and even for the most obscure writings of the 1930s, such as Cantos 52 to 61, which dilate on Chinese dynastic leadership. The mind of beauty can indeed be found in the work of this period, as in these lines from Canto 47:

When the cranes fly high
        think of plowing.

By this gate art thou measured
Thy day is between a door and a door
Two oxen are yoked for plowing
Or six in the hill field
White bulk under olives, a score for drawing down stone,
Here the mules are gabled with slate on the hill road.
Thus was it in time.

Yet, as Moody writes, *The Cantos* were intended to be "the foundation myth of a universal civilization." Pound wanted "to create an epic in which an individual poet would again tell the tale of the tribe, only his tribe would be all of humanity that one man could comprehend; and his tale would be not of himself but would be a universal story, and it would shape a future not for any one nation but for all." As the poet runs off the rails, sparking fragmented rantings, anti-Semitic asides, and a didactic compulsion that mars much of the verse, readers of this book are bound to feel they are watching a slow-motion train wreck.

At every turn, Pound's combination of physical energy and egomania is breathtaking. Moody quotes Caresse Crosby, who with her husband founded the famous Black Sun Press, describing Pound dancing to "a brilliant band of Martinique players" in Paris in 1930:

> As the music grew in fury Ezra avidly watched the dancers. "These people don't know a thing about rhythm" he cried scornfully, and he shut his eyes, thrust forward his red-bearded chin and began a sort of tattoo with his feet—suddenly unable to sit still a minute longer he leapt to the floor and seized the tiny Martinique vendor of cigarettes in his arms, packets flying, then head back, eyes closed, chin out, he began a sort of voodoo prance, his tiny partner held glued against his piston-pumping knees.

His domestic life mixed genuine love and callous indifference. When Dorothy Shakespear, his wife, gave birth to a son by another man, it was Ernest Hemingway who got her to the hospital. Pound immediately adopted the boy, Omar, but was an inattentive father. Mary, his daughter by Olga Rudge, wrote a memoir, *Discretions* (1971), which makes it plain how difficult the Pound family arrangements could be. His messianic focus was on the salvation of art from "this vale of imbecilities." Yet he was not always an elitist. He loved the movies of Walt Disney, and while he had championed Joyce's *Ulysses*, he was less enamored of *Finnegans Wake*: "Nothing short of divine vision or a new cure for the clapp can possibly be worth all the circumambient peripherization."

Somehow in these years, as Pound himself would later admit, he lost sight of the poetry in his own work. After reading the 1,653 pages of Pound's economic manifestoes from the 1930s, Moody makes his own grim assessment: "As the researcher leafs through them the words 'megalomania' and 'doomed' flit through the mind. . . . And whatever happened to his principles of selection and condensation, to the economy of the luminous detail? Was it that his hates, his 'instinct of negation,' knew no bounds?"

Having lost so many close friends in World War I, Pound was desperate to avoid another devastating war. In 1919, he had met the engineer and economic theorist C. H. Douglas, who argued that the modern monetary system encouraged a chronic shortage of purchasing power and did not reflect the real value of a country's labor. He wanted, as Moody summarized Douglas's "Social Credit" theory in the first volume of his biography, to "give the people the purchasing power to buy the things which industry needed to sell" and argued that governments should "distribute credit, not take it away in taxes." Pound became convinced that private banks, by offering credit but siphoning wealth in the form of interest, were draining our cultural energy. If governments made credit freely available, then civilization—meaning art—would prosper. His espousal of Italian fascism had to do not with anti-Semitism, which was not yet part of official Italian policy, but with the belief that Mussolini was a benign dictator who might learn from a poet the true nature of money. Gertrude Stein called Pound "a village explainer, excellent if you were a village, but if you were not, not."

Pound turned a blind eye to Mussolini's increasingly menacing posture, including the invasion of Ethiopia and Italy's role in the Spanish Civil War (1936–39), and he also failed to recognize the even more horrific fascism developing in Germany, with its virulent anti-Semitism. Pound simply saw Germany as another potential model of Social Credit policies. That it was directed by a totalitarian dictator toward bringing on the hell of another war was just another of the terrible contradictions of Pound's activities in the 1930s.

Moody handles these historical complexities superbly, punctuating his narration of Pound's life with passages about the historical developments in Europe. Pound's generalized prejudice against banking dynasties like the Rothschilds became specific and obscene in the 1930s. When a friend protested in a letter that he was going too far, writes Moody, "Pound replied that she should wake up to the real cause of anti-Semitism, 'Get down to USURY / the cause WHY western man vomits out the Jew periodically.' Moreover 'the JEW won't take responsibility for civic order . . . JEW parasite on principle,' and it was necessary to 'Segregate / Quarantine /' as 'defence against parasites,' and in order to resist usury."

The theoretical life had powerfully perverted Pound's thinking. Many of his friends, including the poets Basil Bunting and William Carlos Williams, could see it and warned him to no avail. That Jewish friends like Louis Zukofsky defended him and continued to insist they felt no personal animus from him reminds us how good a friend and attractive a personality Pound could be.

This is what makes Pound the tragic hero of literary Modernism. His accomplishments are undeniable. His generous spirit looms over twentieth-century literature, and in the early years his megalomania seemed harmless. He wanted to be the great poet of history, weaving details from the ancient world, the Middle Ages, the Renaissance, Confucianism, and the Founding Fathers into his increasingly obscure *Cantos*. Moody's book works valiantly to help us see "Pound's method of making music of history." But erudition is not poetry, and many of the cantos fall short as literary imagination. At the same time, the reality of history as it smoldered around him cannot be denied.

In his anguish about the portents of the coming war, Pound traveled to America in 1939 hoping to talk "sense" to politicians. Like Mussolini, they did not take the gadfly poet seriously. His alma mater, Hamilton College, gave him an honorary doctorate in recognition of his literary contributions, yet even there he would not stop defending Mussolini and fascism. He returned to Europe, where "he would deploy such weapons as he had," writes Moody, "words in print, words on the air, words addressed from Italy to America out of the coming war." Ezra Pound's actions, his downfall, and his attempts at redemption all have magnitude. His was a life out of Shakespearean tragedy. As with Lear or Macbeth, we can feel pity as well as horror.

Creating a Literary Hero

JAMES JOYCE

BIOGRAPHIES OF ARTISTS inevitably struggle with blurrings of imagination and fact, and James Joyce presents particular problems on this front, having claimed more than once that he had no imagination at all. A new biography of so brilliant and original a writer—a writer in some cases more admired than loved—also faces the challenge of being compared to Richard Ellmann's magisterial 1959 volume (revised edition 1982). Gordon Bowker's *James Joyce: A New Biography* does not offer any new insight into the artist-hero. That essential narrative of James Joyce is the one we seem to be stuck with, partly because Joyce himself so compellingly created it.

HE CAME FROM the margins.

He had a fine tenor voice and was known as a plausible poet in his home town, a grey imperial backwater of some two hundred thousand souls at the mouth of a river. If there was shame in the decline of his family's fortunes, in the manner of his mother's death at forty-four, in the persistence of his father's drunkenness and the penury of his siblings, particularly his sisters, stranded or sent off to convents, there was also the arrogant willfulness of a young man sure of his vocation and confident of his genius. He had been to Paris and would live there again, and would forge something more in the smithy of his soul than a new version of Irishness. He would make a few books that deserve to be ranked as masterpieces of world literature. He would do this at some cost to himself and others because he believed in heroic effort, but he also believed in the everyday heroism of men nobody noticed, in for example, a middle-age cuckold, another marginal man, a Jewish advertising salesman who saw everything but was seen by no one. Secretive, open, generous, hurt, boyish, ardent, sensual Bloom, bodily Bloom, curious Bloom, grieving Bloom who'd lost a son and whose daughter was out of the house. Here Joyce the father and fantasist could pour forth a fully human creation, and make perhaps the truest hero in modern literature.

And he could go further still, giving us Molly Bloom in her lovely, funny, wild descent into vivid, all-opening sleep. In his final book he infiltrated a world of sleep and dream, the night world, the language of the Unconscious. It is hard to imagine a fuller celebration of word and thing, being and language, than one finds in James Joyce.

JOYCE WAS EXACTING, and scholars of his work have honored that trait by their own obsessions with details. I used to teach in an Irish summer school, and I remember many a day spent in a pub listening to Joyce scholars debate the tiniest detail, down to the milk delivery at such and such an address, one of the eleven homes Joyce experienced in his growing up, as his profligate father squandered funds and uprooted his growing brood to ever more squalid digs. ("The Irishman's house is his coffin," says Bloom, or the *Ulysses* narrator, or both.) With Yeats scholars you would usually just end up reciting verses in ever-more-slurred voices, but with Joyceans the facts were disputed, weighed, interpreted, and if you happened to be in Dublin you would inevitably be taken by the arm, marched up the street and shown where the milk was delivered at the very hour of its delivery. Joyce had told his friend Frank Budgen, "I want to give a picture of Dublin so complete that if the city one day suddenly disappeared from the earth it could be reconstructed out of my book." Joyceans have long taken that statement to heart, pointing out the irony that a city which coldly rejected Joyce, and which he himself rejected and never returned to after 1912, should so completely embrace his legacy now.

ELLMANN HAD THE ADVANTAGE of interviewing many people who had known Joyce well, but he also had a graceful literary sensibility of his own and could fully *imagine* scenes he was writing about. Here, for example, is Ellmann on Joyce's first glimpse of Nora Barnacle, the woman who would so profoundly influence his life and work:

> . . . on June 10, 1904, Joyce was walking down Nassau Street in Dublin when he caught sight of a tall, good-looking young woman, auburn-haired, walking with a proud stride. When he spoke to her she answered pertly enough to allow the conversation to continue. She took him, with his yachting cap, for a sailor, and from his blue eyes thought he might be Swedish.

In the new biography, Bowker touches on the same details, but stands outside them narratively. Instead of staying with the scene, even as briefly as Ellmann does, Bowker immediately associates the moment with Joycean text and offers his interpretation. He also alludes to Brenda Maddox's important biography of Nora:

> Her biographer suggests that probably the myopic Joyce saw only her silhouette and curvaceous movement. But in *Finnegans Wake* there is a hint of something more dramatic—instant sexual magnetism: 'He's fane, she's flirty, with her auburnt streams,

and her coy cajoleries, and her dabblin drolleries, for to rouse his rudderup, or to drench his dreams.'

The passage Bowker quotes is wonderful, and he's certainly not out of bounds in suggesting a direct correlation between biographical fact and Joyce's fiction, but his narrative is less fully imagined in itself, and therein lies a difference between his good book and Ellmann's superb one. This is particularly odd because Bowker avows from the start that he understands his purpose: "Salvaging all the scattered pieces [of evidence] and reassembling them can only produce an approximation of the original, and the drama of ghostly existences will depend on efforts of imagination as much as accumulations of fact."

Peter Costello, author of a very good book on Joyce's early years (*James Joyce: The Years of Growth*, 1992), once told me that Ellmann had made a number of factual errors. Peter saw his book as a corrective. It is certainly a change of emphasis. More weight is given to certain episodes in Joyce's life: his childhood visits to Cork with his father and later efforts to found the first movie theater in Dublin, a business failure that helped seal Joyce's sense of alienation from that city. Costello also frankly produces evidence that on June 16, 1904, Nora Barnacle gave James Joyce a hand job. Joyce had had sex with whores, but this was his first sexual encounter based on affection, and it inspired him, making that date, which we now call Bloomsday, one of the most important in his memory. Ellmann knew about these things, of course, and would edit Joyce's sex-drenched letters to Nora, but in his biography he elected a greater reserve. Call it a defect if you like, but it's really just an omission of details. Joyce's sex life is now common knowledge—or common speculation, since the primary evidence involved is another kind of imaginative literature, *letters*. Bowker's book has nothing really new to offer on this score, if you will; instead, he gives us a synthesis of evidence from other sources: Costello, Brenda Maddox, the letters, etc. That's why this new book exists—not because it can really add to our knowledge of Joyce and his writing, but because it can put between the covers of one book material you would otherwise have to find in scattered sources.

That does make Gordon Bowker's biography a useful one, updating "the life" for new generations of readers. We know that Bloom's sexual fantasies, his epistolary flirtation as Henry Flower, his sadomasochism, his cloacal obsessions, etc., have correlations in the sex life of his creator. But, details aside, didn't we already know that? And is it really illuminating to know it about Joyce when we know it and love it about Bloom? New biographies give us new "facts," but not always new understandings, and I don't think readers of Joyce will understand anything more from the new book than they did from Ellmann and the letters. For all his reference to Joycean texts, all his allusion and quotation, Bowker presents little fresh insight into their meanings. His brief summations of Joyce's fiction are the least compelling passages of his book.

IF ONE IS REALLY going to go whole hog in biographical interpretation, shouldn't one pay more attention to scenes in the fiction itself? In one of the most heartbreaking passages in *Ulysses*, Stephen Dedalus encounters his sister, Dilly, at a bookseller's cart:

> —What are you doing here, Stephen?
> Dilly's high shoulders and shabby dress.
> Shut the book quick. Don't let see.
> —What are you doing? Stephen said.
> A Stuart face of nonesuch Charles, lank locks falling at its sides. It glowed as she crouched feeding the fire with broken boots. I told her of Paris. Late lieabed under a quilt of old overcoats, fingering a pinchbeck bracelet, Dan Kelly's token. *Nebrakada femininum.*
> —What have you there? Stephen asked.

—I bought it from the other cart for a penny, Dilly said, laughing nervously. Is it any good?

My eyes they say she has. Do others see me so? Quick, far and daring. Shadow of my mind.

He took the coverless book from her hand. Chardenal's French primer.

—What did you buy that for? he asked. To learn French?

She nodded, reddening and closing tight her lips.

Show no surprise. Quite natural.

—Here, Stephen said. It's all right. Mind Maggy doesn't pawn it on you. I suppose all my books are gone.

—Some, Dilly said. We had to.

She is drowning. Agenbite. Save her. Agenbite. All against us. She will drown me with her, eyes and hair. Lank coils of seaweed hair around me, my heart, my soul. Salt green death.

We.

Agenbite of inwit. Inwit's agenbite.

Misery! Misery!

There is so much here to explicate and understand. As the eldest surviving child, Stephen has been enthroned as the family prince, just as Joyce was, given advantages none of his siblings shared, especially the girls. This shabby girl, his sister with her high shoulders denoting an anxious posture, has loved her older brother, has heard his tales of Paris. The whole family dynamic is felt here, a painful mix of sympathy and revulsion. She has bought a book she might never be able to use; she too has dreams, has aspirations, and it is horrible that Stephen assumes, probably with some accuracy, that she has no chance of achieving them.

We meet Stephen in *Ulysses* after the bold assertions of *A Portrait of the Artist as a Young Man* have soured. He has returned to Dublin, and following his mother's death is teaching briefly at a school. His trajectory is familiar: like most of his peers he is unable to make a meaningful career in a city of thwarted possibilities, so he wanders from one encounter to another before getting paraplegically pissed and collapsing in the streets, only to be saved by an acquaintance of his father's, the Jewish advertising salesman Leopold Bloom. We know so many of the facts of 1904, so much of the manner of Joyce's composition from memory. Here is Bowker's good description of the method:

> To bring his Edwardian Dublin alive he studied books on period slang, filling pages of his notebooks with words and phrases appropriate to the characters he was now conceiving. When his notebook was not to hand, he made jottings on small scraps of coloured paper, menus and cigarette packets, often forgotten and later discovered in pockets, under ornaments or behind pictures. These notes were entered on to notesheets and, when used, scored in coloured crayon, each colour corresponding to an episode.

But what of the development of sympathies we observe in that bit of dialogue between Stephen and Dilly? Stephen in this scene is not quite the arrogant prig he has been on other occasions. He sees his family drowning and fears he could drown himself, and this deepens our feeling for all involved. It's that level of empathy I miss in Bowker's book. As he himself admits, the facts are not the story.

Biographical detail in Joyce works in much the same way as it does in Dante or Tolstoy, as a way of anchoring both memory and imagination. But it is just as true to say that Joyce's imagination was Catholic in its obsession with symbolic structures, its insistence upon being interpreted.

Bowker quotes Bernard Malamud, from *Dubin's Lives*: "There is no life that can be recaptured wholly; as it was. Which is to say that all biography is ultimately fiction." Fair enough. But the fiction writer's job is to make a world vivid and present to the reader, to make us see, as Conrad put it. Bowker misses opportunities to give us atmosphere and scene. Still, the story deserves retelling. How this man from the margins absorbed so much of his civilization, from the greatest thought to the meanest joke, from opera to the music hall, how he was coddled and disappointed, encouraged in his snobbishness and forced by experience to learn a strain of humility, how he escaped his family and never escaped it, even duplicating his father's alcoholism and profligacy, dying at fifty-eight from a perforated ulcer brought on by his bad habits. How the city of his origins gave him both snobbery and a need to overcome an inferiority complex, not to mention a significant musical and theatrical culture to build upon. How he left that city, first with the hope of returning as a hero, then in bitter disappointment forever. How he worked in terrible conditions, often nearly blind and in physical pain, rarely encouraged by publishers or readers of any sort. How his sympathies and understanding of humanity expanded to the point where he could write the great soliloquy of Molly Bloom, and could understand love as Bloom himself understands it, an utterly embodied tragicomedy that makes us who we are:

—But it's no use, says he. Force, hatred, history, all that. That's not life for men and women, insult and hatred. And everybody knows that it's the very opposite of that that is really life.

Joyce wasn't a fool about it, either, despite the lovely interior whisper: "Folly. Persist." He had seen enough betrayal in Irish history and his friendships with the likes of Oliver St. John Gogarty, the capricious model for Buck Mulligan. He understood the smugness and race-hatred that left Bloom on the margins, the hell-fire sermons of Ireland's clergy, the censoriousness from all quarters that twisted people into stunted caricatures of themselves. The growth of a real artist is indeed a story. And then, of course, a climate of literary opinion was created for him by the likes of Ezra Pound, Harriet Shaw Weaver, Margaret Anderson, and other heroes of Modernism, allowing us to see that the real story is told in the art itself.

When Pound takes the stage in Bowker's book he spikes the prose with his own stage-Yankee vitality: "The katharsis of 'Ulysse', the joyous satisfaction as the first chapters rolled into Holland Place, was to feel that here was the JOB DONE and finished, the diagnosis and cure was here . . . the whole boil of the European mind, had been lanced." Joyce was a character, but the characters who surrounded him are just as stimulating. It's curious that we don't feel more of Nora's presence in this book, that Brenda Maddox's account remains a necessary corrective. The help and sacrifices of others made Joyce's art possible, both by deepening his sympathies as a man and by providing him with money. His long-suffering brother, Stanislaus, who loved and resented him, made it tenable for Joyce and his family to maintain themselves in Trieste and Zurich. And while Pound and other literary friends committed small acts of editorial censorship to get him into print, they also proselytized on his behalf. They built for him the readership he deserved.

None of this would have happened, however, if Joyce had not screwed his courage to the sticking place and completed extraordinary books against enormous odds, twice uprooting his family because of world wars, more often doing so out of economic necessity, battling his own depressions and demons. There was no tenured chair of Creative Writing for James Joyce. There was no Nobel Prize. There was only a life given over to and devoured by the work. That core story remains in all the versions we have of it. Nothing in Bowker's version will alter our admiration for the man who made the books, even if it mildly influences our curiosity about aspects of his sexuality. Bowker's biography is a helpful synthesis of previously existing scholarship. Its value is not that it adds new insight, but that it reminds us once again what real literary ambition can be. I hope it will bring new readers to the beauty and audacity of Joyce's heroic work.

Awe for Auden

W. H. AUDEN, who had seen the jagged edges of war in Spain, China, and Germany, who wrote acutely about strife in poems like "The Shield of Achilles" and "August 1968," who wrote also about love, psychic isolation, and desolating loneliness, believed, despite all he had seen and felt, in "imaginative awe." As he declared in *The Dyer's Hand* (1962), "Poetry can do a hundred and one things, delight, sadden, disturb, amuse, instruct—it may express every possible shade of emotion, and describe every conceivable kind of event, but there is only one thing that all poetry must do; it must praise all it can for being and for happening."

He wasn't a perfect poet, reminding us that, *contra* Yeats, perfection was impossible in both life and art. He was so prolific as an essayist and reviewer that readers are bound to disagree with him now and then. But he left more memorable lines than any other modern poet I can think of, and his prose instructs delightfully on a staggering range of subjects: poetry, fiction, theology, myth, music, drama, philosophy, friendship, sexuality, love, biography—a rare breadth of mind and personality you can actually *learn* from. Confronted with the growing stack of volumes in *The Complete Works of W. H. Auden*, I find myself happy, like a man with his faith restored. The first two editions of his plays, libretti, and other dramatic writings were a mixed bag, to be sure, but now we have six volumes of his prose (the two latest and last having just arrived). Definitive volumes of the verse will complete the series, admirably edited by Edward Mendelson. Here is plenty. Here is one of the major writers of the language. Reading him is both edifying and fun.

Auden was a great aphorist. You can raid his prose for pithy maxims as easily as his verse. Some of his most intriguing essays comprise rearranged snippets from earlier writings. He could forge cogent arguments, but often amused himself making verbal collages, letting a subject live as much in the spaces between sayings as in the sayings themselves. Volume VI of the prose begins with such a kaleidoscope, *A Certain World* (1970), the commonplace book he called "a map of my planet." Instead of composing an autobiography, he assembled favorite writings, organized by topics from "ACCIDIE" and "ACRONYMS" to "BORES," "GOAT, NANNY," "ICEBERGS," and "WORLD, END OF THE." I've never read the book straight through, but over thirty-odd years have occasionally opened it at random, finding new curiosities, such as Abraham Cowley's praise of lettuce (under the heading "PLANTS"):

> You are indeed a useful medicine to all tyrants, and madness flees when touched with your divine coolness. Gird, I pray you, their heads with a better crown; and, if you can, bring succour through them to this world. At your command, love, the greatest of tyrants, sometimes abandons inflamed hearts. It is a false love, for you do not attempt to expel true love, which has the title of a just king and deserves to be loved. That dog-star lust which slays green things with its fire and gives birth to monsters is rightly hated by you.

Salad will never be the same.

Fittingly, *A Certain World* ends with "WRITING," returning Auden to the one subject on which he unabashedly claimed expertise:

What the poet has to convey is not "self expression," but a view of a reality common to all, seen from a unique perspective, which it is his duty as well as his pleasure to share with others. To small truths as well as great, St. Augustine's words apply.

"The truth is neither mine nor his nor another's; but belongs to us all whom Thou callest to partake of it, warning us terribly, not to account it private to ourselves, lest we be deprived of it."

No entry on "TRUTH" appears in the book, but this sense of shared reality is refreshing in our fractious times. Auden writes about faith in ways an agnostic like myself can appreciate, and even when he's laying down the law I sense bemusement more than hectoring.

Perhaps the best a reviewer of these books can do is to make a little commonplace book out of Auden's prose, knowing the selections would change over years of re-reading. What follows are my own snippets and clippings and comments of the moment, offered for pleasure and instruction as well as the glimpse they give into the gold these books contain.

Friends, Poetic

We know from "In Memory of W. B. Yeats" that Auden was one of the great elegists. His prose eulogies for friends like Louis MacNeice, T. S. Eliot, and Louise Bogan are stuffed with memorable anecdote and insight. Thinking in 1963 of MacNeice, who had died at fifty-five of pneumonia, he was moved to profundity:

Our mortality is seldom real to us. Even when our parents die, our primary awareness is not so much of death as of loneliness—henceforth we shall no longer be sustained by a bond which, because it was created by nature, could not be broken: from now on, our relations with others will depend, for better or worse, upon their choice and ours. But when a person of our own generation to whom we have been close, as a brother, a husband, a lover, a friend, a colleague, someone we have opened our hearts to and shared our thoughts with, someone with whom we have frequently drunk and joked together, dies suddenly, our sorrow is accompanied by terror—instead of our friend, the dead man might be you or I and, if it were so, to how many, in truth, would our absence be real? For when death is really present to us, we cannot deceive ourselves.

He has plenty of specific memories about MacNeice as a man and poet—the happiest of them being their journey together in Iceland in 1936—but it's typical of Auden to extract general truths from experience, and on the subjects of love, friendship, and death he always wrote beautifully:

> We all know what the word *love* ought to mean, for we all know how we should like to be loved—for ourselves as we are—but it is difficult, perhaps impossible, to love the living as we ought, because our relation to them is confused and corrupted by our own selfish envies, hopes and fears. To the degree, however, that our love for the living has been genuine, our love for the dead, in relation to whom there is no distinction between past and future, can, with God's grace, become perfect, without desire, without competition.

What would MacNeice want of his friends at such a time, Auden wonders. His answer is civility itself:

> Firstly, surely, that, remembering him and for his sake, we should more than ever enjoy those temporal pleasures which he can no longer share with us, his pleasure in language, in country landscapes, in city streets and parks, in birds, beasts and flowers, in nice clothes, good conversation, good food, good drink, and in what he called "the tangles".

Secondly, that we may always find the strength to be ourselves, which, since we are not animals but human beings, means to be reborn every day.

One can quibble here: aren't animals more perfectly reborn every day than humans with their interfering egos? But the lesson Auden offers like the gentlest Sunday School teacher is nonetheless welcome. He gets you thinking.

Auden also wrote a superb verse elegy for MacNeice, "The Cave of Making," in which a writer's desk resembles "Weland's Stithy," a forge and a site of alchemy: "Here silence / is turned into objects." The writer's interior space cannot deny what lies beyond it: "More than ever / life-out-there is goodly, miraculous, lovable, / but we shan't, not since Stalin and Hitler, / trust ourselves ever again: we know that, subjectively, / all is possible." Both Auden and MacNeice disliked literary aesthetes, and were always inclined to underplay the efficacy of poetry in the world:

> After all, it's rather a privilege
> amid the affluent traffic
> to serve this unpopular art which cannot be turned into
> background noise for study
> or hung as a status trophy by rising executives,
> cannot be "done" like Venice
> or abridged like Tolstoy, but stubbornly still insists upon
> being read or ignored: our handful
> of clients at least can rune.

When Auden declares in the prose eulogy that his friend "was totally lacking" in the "vanity and envy" infecting so many other writers, I believe him. Auden spent his life earning our trust by writing well and precisely, even ejecting several strong poems from his canon because he thought them untrue. He's never pious, never self-aggrandizing, often funny and utterly down-to-earth. Many of these essays display more frankness about his homosexuality than you might have thought possible for the time. In the case of MacNeice, a lover of women, Auden takes care to honor his friend's character and art: "Louis Mac-Neice was clearly a poet who shared Cesar Pavese's belief that 'the only joy in life is to begin', that, from the poet's point of view, the excitement of tackling a problem, whether of technique or subject matter, which one has never attempted before, is even more important than the result."

Writing about Eliot, he is moved to consider what makes a poet great. One sign, he argues, is that if he declared "Marina" to be Eliot's best poem there would be "an internal clamor of dissent" in which equally valuable candidates were named, "until I realize I am thankful to have read everything Eliot wrote, even those poems which do not appeal to me very much." The other sign of Eliot's greatness, Auden writes, is that while he cannot predict how many pages in future anthologies would be devoted to his work, "I am quite certain that something of his will be there."

We cannot know, of course, but it's a measure of his magnitude that I feel the same about Auden.

Friends, Non-Poetic

I lost count of the poets written about in these volumes, from the ancient Greeks to Goethe, Byron, Cavafy, Housman, and Larkin, but Auden's interests were wide, and he numbered among his friends many who were not artists, including U.N. Secretary-General Dag Hammarskjöld, who was killed in a plane crash in 1961 on his way to cease-fire negotiations in the Congo. I remember in my childhood seeing Hammarskjöld's diary, *Markings*, in many households. I may even have received a copy of it as a gift, but I don't recall reading it. Auden's Fore-word to the book is remarkable for its candor:

My own testimony is unimportant, but I want to give it. Brief and infrequent as our meetings were, I loved the man from the moment I saw him. His knowledge and understanding of poetry, the only field in which I was competent to judge the quality of his mind, were extraordinary, and, presumptuous as it sounds, I felt certain of a mutual sympathy between us, of an unexpressed dialogue beneath our casual conversation. The loneliness and the religious concern which his diary records, I sensed; indeed, I think the only two things which, while translating it, came as a real surprise, were his familiarity with the Anglican Psalter, and his fascination with the haiku as a poetic form.

Auden respected men and women of action, people of good works like Dorothy Day. "Wherever real social evil exists," he wrote in another essay, "poetry, or any of the arts for that matter, is useless as a weapon. Aside from direct political action, the only weapon is factual reportage—photographs, statistics, eye-witness reports."

Yet the awareness of evil, the social and religious consciousness I find in many of his poems, is a weapon too, despite his modest claims. Great poetry arms the psyche of those who encounter it. Poetry lives, as he says more than once in these volumes, only when it encounters a reader.

A later review of a book about Hammarskjöld contains this parenthesis: "Incidentally, I met Chou En-lai in Hankow in 1938, and am very happy to find that Hammarskjöld's high opinion of him confirms my own impression. The three politicians I have met in my life whom I most admire are Hammarskjöld, Chou En-lai, and Teddy Kollek, the Mayor of Jerusalem." Not many poets could make a statement like that, arising from the realm of action rather than contemplation. Auden inhabited his century on multiple levels, an unwilling but necessary prophet.

Hammarskjöld won a posthumous Nobel Peace Prize, while Auden remains in the honorable *salon des refusés* for the literature award. These two facts are connected, as Mendelson reports in his introduction to Volume V:

> Auden had been Hammarskjöld's candidate for the Nobel Prize. In 1963, when George Seferis won the prize, Auden was one of three finalists, and was widely expected to win in 1964. Then, in the spring of that year, Hammarskjöld's executors and his friends in the diplomatic service were horrified and offended by Auden's introduction when they read it in typescript. A high Swedish official visited Auden in New York and hinted that the Swedish Academy would be distressed if his introduction should be printed as written. Auden refused to rewrite it, and that evening, said to his friend Lincoln Kirstein, "There goes the Nobel Prize."

Auden had gently alluded to Hammarskjöld's homosexuality and tendency to narcissism, and was not about to lie for literary favor.

Lives, Private

His dislike of literary biography is well known. He shuddered at the thought of having his letters published or being the subject of a "life." But he made careful exceptions. Reviewing a book about Wagner, he refuses to forgive the great composer for his virulent anti-Semitism, adding,

> . . . I do not believe that an artist's life throws much light upon his works. I do believe, however, that, more often than most people realize, his works may throw light upon his life.

In a long review for *The New Yorker* (3 April 1965), Auden takes up the memoirs of two very different men: Leonard Woolf and Evelyn Waugh. "If not in complete accord with

either, I feel myself sufficiently close to Mr. Waugh theologi-
cally and to Mr. Woolf politically to act as a moderator." He
then intersperses narrations from his two subjects with some
of his most revealing autobiographical prose. Comparing his
experience of World War I to those of his elders, Waugh and
Woolf, Auden remembers the feeling of loss when, at age seven,
he saw his father depart as a medical officer. He would not see
his father again for another seven years. I am struck by Auden's
honesty here in his writing about school life, homosexuality, and even his drinking habits, which had become as prodi-
gious and addictive as Waugh's. He never mentions that Waugh
detested him and his friend Christopher Isherwood for their
sexuality and for their having left England in 1939, just before
World War II. If charity can be shown, Auden is usually the
one showing it.

Writing about eighteenth-century figures Sydney Smith and
Alexander Pope, he commends the first for taking "short views
of human life—not further than dinner or tea" as a method
of combating depression. Pope is admirable in that "he never
became an aesthete—never, that, is, regarded his vocation as
superior to all others."

In other words, Auden's contempt for biographical data
does not prevent him from extracting lessons about behavior
from them. His denials of biographical legitimacy were contradictory and psychologically complex. In one of his essays on
Kierkegaard he asserts, "The question 'Is X a good or bad poet?'
and the question 'Is X a good or bad husband?' have nothing to
do with each other." But writing in the Foreword to *Secondary Worlds* (1967), his "T. S. Eliot Memorial Lectures" delivered
at the University of Kent, he explains, "The relation between
those secondary worlds which we call works of art and the
primary world of our everyday social experience is a problem
which concerns every artist. . . ." The problem took up a lot of
his intellectual and imaginative life—in his elegies, in his more
personal poems, and in much of the prose collected here. He's

not above laughing about it, either, when he says at the start of one review: "This excellent compilation happens to be dedicated to me, but I am not going to allow the honor to stop me from log-rolling."

Quotations, Arbitrary

"A true enchantment: the enchanted one only desires that the enchanting being shall continue to exist, independent and irrespective of his own existence. A false enchantment: the enchanted one desires either to possess or be possessed by the enchanting being, to become either its master or its slave."

"Health is the state about which Medicine has nothing to say. Holiness is the state about which Theology has nothing to say."

"The notion of the alienated artist is a phenomenon of the second half of the nineteenth century. In earlier times we do not find it and, in our own, alienation has become almost a universal problem."

"I myself have taken mescaline once and L.S.D. once. Aside from a slight schizophrenic dissociation of the I from the Not-I, including my body, nothing happened at all."

". . . when I watch or read a Greek tragedy, I identify myself with the chorus, never with the hero."

Religion and Art

Reviewing a collection of essays by the classicist E. R. Dodds, Auden notes their range and diversity: "This makes the task of a reviewer very difficult, since each chapter deserves a review to itself." I feel precisely the same way about the essays, introductions, and reviews collected in these two volumes, and to say something sufficient about the religious life running through them would require a dissertation.

Auden returned to the church in 1940. He was living in New York, dealing with the death of his mother, the betrayal of his lover, Chester Kallman, and the hideously obvious problem of evil at work in the world. He wrote about these things in many different works, some of them found here. An aphoristic essay called "Behaviour, Action and Enchantment" (1965) puts the issue of religious conversion or return this way:

> Everyone who has been brought up as a Christian has to make the transition from the child's *We believe still* to the adult's *I believe again.*
>
> This transition can never at any time have been easy, and in our age it is rarely made without a hiatus, short or long, of disbelief.

Auden's hiatus was saturated with psychology and politics, and religion provided a means for observing the ego's involvement in those realms.

Unlike Eliot's, his Christianity was untainted by anti-Semitism. Reviewing another book by Dodds, he expressed what seem to me highly civilized views of the place of religion in public life,

> As an Episcopalian, I do not believe that Christianity did triumph or has triumphed. Thus, while I consider the fourth-century victory of Christian doctrine over Neoplatonism, Manicheism, Gnosticism, Mithraism, etc., to have been what school history books used to call "a good thing," I consider the adoption of Christianity as the official State religion, backed by the coercive powers of the State, however desirable a thing it may have seemed at the time, to have been a "bad," that is to say, an unchristian thing.

The current erosion of the separation of Church and State in this country would have appalled him, as would the continued use of religious beliefs all over the world as excuses for murder.

The *place* of religion, like the *place* of art, is a matter of individual and private choice, as he wrote for the BBC in 1966:

> When we turn from political action to the making and enjoying of works of art, we find ourselves, in a very different world. In the first place, art (science, too, for that matter), is a gratuitous activity. Nobody can be compelled to write a poem and nobody is obliged to read one. Thus, while social-political history is continuous—at every moment some kind of society is in being, some political event occurring, so that the only alternative to one kind of society or event would be another— the history of art is discontinuous—to *this* work of art there are two alternatives: another work or no work at all.

The place of morality is not a matter of judging another, but of understanding the existence of evil and the consequences of human actions. Auden brings science and morality powerfully together in "The Corruption of Innocent Neutrons," his piece for the *New York Times Magazine* (1 August 1965) on the twentieth anniversary of Hiroshima. And in writing about "Good and Evil in *The Lord of the Rings*" (Auden had been a student of Tolkien's at Oxford and was devoted to the Hobbit books) he makes moral and theological distinctions:

> In the Primary World we are all aware of our deplorable tendency, when our interests, still more than the interests of our social group, come into conflict with others, to identify our cause with Good and that of our enemies with Evil. There have been Just Wars: most of us would agree that it was as morally necessary for England and the United States to resist Germany and Japan by force of arms as it was for Rohan and Gondor to resist the armies of Saruman and Sauron. Individual men can be wicked: Hitler was not another Sauron, but he seems to have come as close to being one as is possible for a mortal. It would, however, be grossly unjust to say that all Germans and Japanese, even the majority, were wicked.

He once wrote of Eliot, "A major poet and a good man has just died." In Auden's case, the "goodness" seems even more apparent, if unclaimed.

Word, The Last

Auden's advice to students encountering Byron for the first time: "Before you attempt to read any of the poetry, read *all* of the prose, his letters and journals. Once you have read these, you will be able, when you come to the poems, to recognize immediately which are the authentic and which are bogus." I would not give the same advice to students freshly encountering Auden. One needs to be enchanted and mystified by the poems first—"Lullaby," "Law Like Love," "As I Walked Out One Evening," "Musée des Beaux Arts," "Orpheus," "Miss Gee," "In Time of War," "Atlantis," "In Praise of Limestone".... I give up, as all list-makers must when confronted with genius. Read the poems first. Dwell with them a while. And read the prose for its own sake—for the expansive, compassionate mind, the humor, the offered companionship. Take Auden whole, as best you can. The Princeton edition of his *Complete Works* is making that possible for the first time.

Praise

The Name Inside the Name

KEVIN HART

W<small>HEN WE ENCOUNTER</small> a superb poet for the first time, we re-learn how to listen, how to read. In Eliot's words, it is "a new beginning, a raid on the inarticulate / With shabby equipment always deteriorating. . . ."

We were in Oregon, driving north on Highway 101, and my wife was telling me about Kevin Hart, a poet and scholar whom she had known in Australia and whom we had just met briefly at a conference in Pennsylvania. She opened her iPad as I drove, located some Hart poems on line and began to read: "There is a silence words can't touch."

If I thought anything then it might have been: "Good line. Not great. Good." Most poets endure mixed feelings about their medium. The extraordinary plenitude of language and the poverty of our efforts. The second line quickened my interest: "And there's a name inside my name. . . ." I wasn't thinking about a heart having a Hart inside it. Not yet. Nor did I know that Hart's mother was Jewish, though she kept that identity hidden, and that he would have been thinking of the secret Hebrew name Jews traditionally have written inside their proper name.

The poem was called "My Name," and with time I would discern that Kevin Hart often repeats the same tropes, obsessively getting at elusive experience behind or beyond or within them. Name. Emerson said the poet is a namer. Name and nature. The nominal and the numinous, the spirit ground where word and experience nearly meet, where poet and reader gaze across an open field. To name, to nominate, to suggest, to evoke, to invoke. One falls down a rabbit hole in reading.

Here, from *Wild Track: New and Selected Poems*, is the whole poem I heard in my wife's Australian accent that summer morning:

> There is a silence words can't touch.
> And there's a name inside my name
> Though one my mother never said out loud
>
> She never said it, never once, although
> She knew there was another name
> That sleeps inside my name.
>
> *Sleep now, old name,*
> *For no one wants to know of you*
>
> My mother, she is dead these dozen years
> And she is grown so small
> She sleeps inside my name when it is said
>
> I think she sleeps
> Within that other name as well, more deeply, far
> More quietly, turning only once or twice
> Inside that paradise
>
> *Sleep now, old love,*
> *It is too late to say a word to you*

By the end of it we were wiping away tears. "Read it again," I said. With each hearing I became more aware that its sure-footed technique and apparent simplicity were enacting not only personal grief, but also the very condition and purpose of poetry itself. The place where being and poetry appear to be one and the same. As I came to know more of Hart's poetry—teaching one of his collections and inviting him to my college to lecture and read—I realized how rare and profound it is. Our trivializing age can hardly apprehend such beauty, or connect poetry's expressions of the inexpressible to a true evocation of being.

Notice how nothing in this poem is wasted, nothing is extraneous. Nothing shows off the poet's studiousness or cleverness—even though these words were written by one of the most erudite intellectuals on the planet. How each line moves the poem further into knowledge and the limits of knowledge. What would a name inside a name be? What psychological or spiritual or linguistic conditions are nominated there? A whole flood of them—all at once. Line three introduces a mother in particular relation to the name. One thinks of Yeats: "Our part / To murmur name upon name / As a mother names her child."

My wife is a namer, a poet, and a mother. When she sees into a person she loves, she gives that person a new name. Hart's mother—or the mother in the poem—never says the name she knows. The quality of knowledge is ambiguous, but the personal reserve of a certain kind of Englishwoman also comes into play. And what of the name? It "sleeps inside my name." An infant slumber, a dream state, a liminal ambiguity.

We're six lines into the poem when Hart makes the first turn. His form of address has been declarative, simple, lucid, and has already opened up imaginal caverns, when he turns to address the name in a tone of forgiving grief and resignation and acceptance all in one quiet imperative chord:

Sleep now, old name,
For no one wants to know of you

This is a lullaby, eulogy, and invocation. There's the grief of having been unknown, unnamed, unseen, or having the fact of one's being seen move off in distances of death and sleep. By writing in more than one voice—declarative, imperative—Hart dissolves unity of being and breaks our hearts. The imaginal, the numinous—all these locations of the unsayable—nod toward a place where poetry and religion meet.

Hart writes as a practicing Catholic whose philosophical and theological writings explore kinds of skepticism and deconstruction. I read as an agnostic with virtually no formal religious training and none of his intellectual equipment. Yet his technique makes new understandings and sympathies possible for me. Unlike most contemporary poetry I read, Hart's writing enlarges my experience rather than diminishing it.

Look at his fourth stanza, the move in its opening line. Having addressed the "old name," he names "My mother." The comma presents another turn, another space for motion and emotion before the sad declaration, "she is dead these dozen years." Then the surreal reality of such presences: "And she is grown so small / She sleeps inside my name when it is said." There is relation and relationship in what is said and what cannot be said. Death and the imaginal are both hermetic—they involve doorways.

Notice Hart's lines and endings. The poem contains several lovely pentameters and one hexameter, but also shorter scanable lines that do not feel like prosaic contemporary free verse. Hear the penultimate stanza again with a pause after each line, and hear the unnameable doubleness in his rhyme:

I think she sleeps [pause]

Within that other name as well, more deeply, far [pause]

More quietly, turning only once or twice [pause]

Inside that paradise [pause]

We feel grace even as we fall from it, and turn again to his final imperative:

Sleep now, old love,
It is too late to say a word to you

"God is beyond the reach of language," Hart has said in a radio interview (Australian Broadcasting Corporation, January 13, 2015). But so are poetry's most common subjects, love and death. Religion and poetry remain deeply related, not in the doctrines and prejudices of orthodoxy or anti-orthodoxy, but in the open field of being. Poetry is making, but it is also reaching and the attempt to reach, and even for non-believers it is close to prayer.

Hart's compatriot and fellow Catholic poet Les Murray writes in "Poetry and Religion," "Nothing's said till it's dreamed out in words / and nothing's true that figures in words only" (*New Selected Poems* 84). But as Murray says in another poem, "Nothing's free when it's explained" (112). A critic's position before real poetry is like the awe-struck botanist in a rain forest. Ultimately one can only point and name and wonder.

I FIRST HEARD Kevin Hart speaking on a panel devoted to "Poetry and Religion." I walked in late, just as he was answering a question about prayer. A tall, slender man whose demeanor beams intelligence, he sat back in his chair, raised his spectacled eyes and spread his arms—not in figurative crucifixion, but in a demonstration of self-exposure, the complete opening of oneself to God. This vulnerability toward otherness, however we conceive it, arises from courage that can seem to others reckless. Never sentimental in his poetry, Hart does not guard himself from emotion. This puts him at a remove from much contemporary poetry, which remains locked in adolescence, wanting to belong but never venturing beyond the tropes and truisms of particular cliques. Like all the best poets,

Hart does not converse with his time only, but also with the past, as Yeats wanted to dine "With Landor and with Donne." Hart can be read with the Metaphysicals, with Teresa of Avila and John of the Cross, with Hopkins and Eliot, yet he feels quietly original and utterly unpretentious.

The best poetry lives through expressions of the inexpressible, the uncanny, and Hart seems to me one of the best poets of our time partly by standing both outside it and inside it, by being a poet of liminal states like imagination, desire, and religious feeling. His materials are the ordinary world of family, romantic and sexual love, fatherhood and childhood. His forms are often simple, regularly iambic, aiming to present no unnecessary challenges to our comprehension. My students adored his poetry. Many of them chose to memorize and recite it in class. His simplicity is not deceptive so much as it is revelatory, full of openings between the lines. He resembles and is often compared to the French poet Yves Bonnefoy in his lucidity, his turns and returns, his lush but quiet lyricism.

Born in England in 1954, Hart spent his first dozen years feeling like a failure and an idiot. He did not get on well at school, did not understand his lessons, and remembers looking at mathematics problems as a code he would never break. At one point his mother took him to a butcher, hoping he could apprentice to that trade since nothing else was working out for him. In 1966 he immigrated with his family to Brisbane, Australia, and it was there, a teenaged boy in a mathematics classroom, that a window opened suddenly and he experienced something like the Grace of God—an epiphany. He could suddenly *see* and understand what was before him. Rapidly he went from bottom to top of his class, became a math whiz, and fell in love with poetry and girls. He memorized Shelley's "Ozymandias" for an assignment, then read all of Shelley and from there proceeded to Hopkins and Eliot.

Hart's family was not particularly religious, but the young poet and scholar found his own road to religion, first through the poetry of Baptist hymns, and eventually to Roman Catholicism with its traditions of contemplation and the *lectio divina*. He took a BA at the Australian National University in Canberra, where he studied with and befriended A. D. Hope, a poet who modeled both intellectual rigor and *joie de vivre*—a delightfully apolitical randiness and celebration of the body. Hart earned his PhD at the University of Melbourne and taught comparative literature at nearby Monash University, moving in 2002 to Notre Dame in the United States. Currently he is Professor of Christian Studies in the religion department at the University of Virginia, with courtesy chairs, for good measure, in English and French. He also holds a chair in philosophy at the Australian Catholic University in Melbourne.

Hart has published widely in philosophy, literary theory, and theology, including work on Maurice Blanchot, Jacques Derrida, and Jean-Luc Marion. His background in ideas and languages allows him to clarify fields that have long been muddied by lesser minds. Where some would find no common ground between deconstruction and religion, Hart reminds us of deconstruction's origins in scripture and the words of Martin Luther. He uses apophatic theology, the *via negativa*, as a mode of deconstruction. As he put it in the radio interview I cited earlier, we can "question the predications of things." The spiteful negatives of absolutists dissolve in the presence of such clear thinking, a mind that can connect scripture and theory. He cites Paul in I Corinthians 1:19: "For it is written, I will destroy the wisdom of the wise, and will bring to nothing the understanding of the prudent." Hart finds the Old Testament antecedent for this passage in Isaiah 29:14: "Therefore, behold, I will proceed to do a marvelous work and a wonder, for the wisdom of their wise men shall perish, and the understanding of their prudent men shall be hid" (both quotations KJV).

The religious encounter and the critical and philosophical encounters become nearly indistinguishable in phenomenological terms—in how we read and how we experience. As

Robert Frost put it, "The figure is the same as for love." We long to name and be named, know and be known, but in life as in art we remain in process, in motion, blessedly and tortuously and lastingly unachieved.

Echoing the mystical relations of St. John of the Cross and T. S. Eliot, Hart talks of the Divine longing for us even as we desire to know the Divine. The relationship is at some level erotic. "The figure is the same as for love." John of the Cross encounters his beloved in "*la noche dichosa*," which John Frederick Nims translates as "the lucky dark" (*Poems of St. John of the Cross* 18–19).

"Desire moves," Anne Carson reminds us. "Eros is a verb" (*Eros the Bittersweet* 17). Whether metaphor or metaphysics, Eros is directional, relational, and allows us to experience through the senses that which we cannot see or name. St. John of the Cross wrote of "union with God by the way of spiritual negation," and went out "to where there waited one / I knew—how well I knew!— / in a place where no one was in view."

Hart is a frankly erotic poet. In a sequence entitled "Sugar" he writes, "Today I want a life / That's sweet, without a thought," and launches into celebratory sex. The world is fully animated: "A storm lets down its hair / But no one's climbing up: / We're staying in today / And making love, I hope. . . ." Ecstasy is what it is, and it is always more than one thing:

> Let's fuck in French today,
> *Mon sucre:* kiss
> Me thinking lacy things
> In *Marseillais, Suisse,*
>
> Or any tongue you like!

Eros is too rare in contemporary poetry, as is joy, as is any strong emotion. This is the delight of Donne, the wonder that obliterates the wise, the canticle that became the Song of Songs.

HART'S EROTIC SEQUENCE is the final poem in *Wild Track: New and Selected Poems* (2015), and it concludes with mixed feelings:

You stupid rain, fat rain,
No one likes you!
The baby sparrows cry
Cars splash away

You trashy lowlife rain
Stomping on grass
And in small nests too full
No one likes you!

Old broken tattered rain
Hard-working rain
In the mushy garden
Well, maybe stay

Sweet rain, o kindly rain,
Doodle all day
Chill until evening comes
Keep sugar here

The moods change as registers of diction change—that "Chill" both noun and slang imperative verb. That sweetness in "Keep sugar here," knowing we never can *carpe diem* without surrendering to it.

One marvel about Hart is his access to multiple ages. He can summon up childhood, adolescence, and the advancing years with equal facility. Consider a late "Lullaby," one of two poems he has dedicated to his dead sister, Marion:

Ah lully, lully, butterbones,
Your mother's put you in my hands
And gone away to peel the stones:
    Nobody understands.

Ah lully, lully, feathercrown,
Why all these big hot tears tonight?
The sky has holes, thin rain runs down,
    Your father's lost his light.

Ah lully, lully, kick'n'shove,
The world is dark indeed, my dear,
I rock you in the darkness, love,
    And wish that you were here.

Ah lully, lully, little ears,
Our parents both have said adieu—
And you've been dead these sixty years:
    Now I must carry you.

We're taken back to the name within a name, to psychic origins, embodiments of being and grief.

Grief gives meaning to joy and joy to grief, and both are passages we live. Taking his cue from negative theology, Hart has developed in his poetry a relationship to a God he cannot name, using euphemisms like "Dark One" to save himself from sentimental associations with goodness and light. Here, returning to the family, is one of many poems for his father, "Morning Knowledge," in which morning has its usual double meaning:

My gentle father died when day was young,
When there was very little left to take;
Gray face, a raft of bones, a bitter ache,
A word or two still living on my tongue.

There's bread that only dying men can eat,
Worn words that only weary men can say.
Sometimes those wispy words just slip away,
Sometimes the gritty bread falls on a sheet.

In those last days my dad ate nothing much;
His words were mostly gnawing at warm air.

Dark One, I'll be the one to smooth his hair.
You be the one who lets him know my touch.

The simple iambics and envelope stanzas offer perhaps too firm a closure, yet the last two lines of this remarkable poem enact the actuality of death. I can touch my dead father's hair, but whatever realm he has crossed over to—face to face with God or leafing out in some other cell-life—he is beyond the realm where the material of my words or my touch would seem to matter.

This is the kind of profundity-within-simplicity we find in poets like Blake, and Hart does it without a trace of self-aggrandizement. His voice is strong and humble, which is not to say he is always quiet:

Dark Bird

What do you want with me today, dark bird?
Why are you flying low, beneath that branch?
I know your shadow: you were long since gone,
My killdeer, rough-winged swallow, mourning dove,

Death plays its flute with all your bones, dark bird,
You brood within my nest of breath, dark bird,
Your razor claw is in my eye, dark bird,
Sweet finches are in blossom here, dark bird,

My father's dying now, dark bird, you know,
He feels your shadow now, dark bird, you know,
His bones are hollow now, dark bird, you know,
He's turned to feathers now, dark bird, you know,

Take to another land, dark bird, fly now,
Go snap sweet sunflower souls, dark bird, fly now,
A thousand deaths await you there, dark bird,
Fly fast dark bird fly fast fly past dark bird

HART'S SCHOLARSHIP is a professional excellence of its own, and much of it works at the knot of negative theology and deconstruction, the phenomenology of mysticism at the core of his poetry. Here I am frankly out of my element, working from scant reading and my own intuition. It seems to me important that Hart has written in books like *The Dark Gaze* not only about such figures as Derrida, but also the novelist and philosopher Maurice Blanchot, a lapsed Catholic who explores "the experience of the absence of God."

> Heidegger warned us decades ago that the absence of God is "not nothing" but on the contrary is the fullness of a vast and complex heritage, and even earlier he had said that "The flight of the gods must be experienced [*erfahren*] and endured." If Blanchot interprets this experience by way of atheism, he acknowledges that the deity returns as a ghost in the assumptions of philosophy and in the reserve on which literature calls.

Unlike some thinkers who look only for confirmation of what they already believe, Hart remains a Catholic who wants to understand other positions, particularly the problem of language. He writes, "I do not follow the strain of 'religion without religion' that passes from Kant through Blanchot and finds a distinguished contemporary expositor in Jacques Derrida. . . ." He still has to understand the relational terms of an I and a Thou when neither can be asserted with confidence, as well as the difference between being and belief. There is common and humanizing ground here for the believer and the unbeliever, if they will consent to listen to each other.

His scholarly study, *The Dark Gaze: Maurice Blanchot and the Sacred* (2004), is too complete an intellectual history for me to paraphrase here, but I can at least notice a few passages that illuminate Hart's poetry. I'm particularly drawn to his chapter connecting Blanchot to Bonnefoy, who "asks us to consider that those eminent human possibilities, art and religion, both respond to an obscure dimension that precedes all gods and most certainly the God of the monotheistic faiths. This realm is impossible to name since it is neither phenomenon nor noumenon, and perhaps the best we can do is to dub it 'the impossible.'"

Poets find perverse comfort in this "impossible," but ought to know they share the place with thinkers in other fields. Philosophy and poetry were not always so easy to tell apart, and still recognize each other like sleepy lovers waking after a mistaken night. Sometimes theology wakes in the same bed.

W. H. Auden slyly jokes about "The poet, / Admired for his earnest habit of calling / The sun the sun, his mind a Puzzle . . ." (*Selected Poems* 191). Skepticism about the efficacy of language has been built into poetry for a very long time, and both philosophy and theology are enlivened, it would seem, when they encounter poetic doubts in poetic terms. Touching on religion, Hart quotes a poem by Bonnefoy, then offers it in Richard Pevear's translation:

> We no longer see each other in the same light,
> We no longer have the same eyes or the same hands.
> The tree is closer, the voice of the springs more lively,
> Our steps are deeper now, among the dead.
>
> God who are not, put your hand on our shoulder,
> Sketch out our body with the weight of your return,
> Complete the mixing of our souls with these stars,
> These woods, these bird-calls, these shadows, these days.
>
> Renounce yourself in us as a fruit bursts open,
> Blot us out in you. Unveil for us
> The mysterious meaning of what is all so simple
> And would have burnt darkly in loveless words.

It's the relational moment, when a nonexistent God is asked to "put your hand on our shoulder," that comes close to Hart's own practice. He believes, but he knows the distance opened up between his words and his belief. All devotional poetry has a problem, in that it uses the material of words to approach the sacred. That's why so much of it, from Hafez to Herbert to Hart, is couched in dramatic encounters, arguments, rebellions, resistances, lapses, hangovers.

The poem is a substance, but it is not the sacred itself. In the course of his reading, Hart remembers Wordsworth, the poet's desire for a language that connects:

> Language, if it do not uphold, and feed, and leave in quiet, like the power of gravitation or the air we breathe, is a counter-spirit, unremittingly and noiselessly at work to derange, to subvert, to lay waste, to vitiate, and to dissolve.

It must be both spirit and counter-spirit, presence and absence, part of what Hart calls "infinite conversation," alluding to the title of a book by Blanchot. In the face of wonder, the wisdom of the wise shall perish.

Hart seems always to have understood the relationship of language and the sacred to be dynamic and changing, involved in the imaginal, as he suggests in a poem called "Approaching Sleep":

> Footsteps in the attic, those crooked sounds
> You hear at night, the train's blind whistle, or
> Dead letters slipped beneath your bedroom door,
>
> And still there is your heart that beats upon
> Your ear and fills you as you lie in bed;
> It beats and beats but cannot keep good time
>
> And lets it drop like water from a tap.
> You write a letter of complaint to God
> While half-asleep, forgetting the address.
>
> Outside, the night is wide as a winter lake
> After the heavy rains, and it is June
> With days that open like a Chinese box.

If anything is real, it is the mind
Approaching sleep, listing the tiny bones
Within the ear: *anvil, stirrup, hammer* . . .

The surgeon placed them on a woman's watch,
The seconds crudely sweeping underneath.
Within my ear, a fine Dutch miniature

With cool canals, a blacksmith by his horse,
A small boy playing on a smaller drum,
Old women who darn their shadows against each dusk.

There is a monster in the labyrinth
But still behind you, walking when you walk:
It is too late to get out now, the watch

You hold up to your ear stopped long ago;
That angry letter you wrote to God returns
Addressed to you, but now means something else.

This is our between-ness, which can be a heaven or a hell at just the slightest change of inflection. The delight in human connection, in sex and love, carries with it the shadow griefs, absence and loss, eternally.

If we love poetry, often it is due to our experience of the ephemeral simultaneously with notions of the eternal, the airy nothing of a self stirred by overwhelming currents of life and death. Call it God or call it "God who are not," we never escape the ecstasy and pain of our relation to it. By the same token, poetry is an art of ambiguous relation—utterly betrayed when treated as position paper or criticism or mere politics. It is that "raid on the inarticulate" Eliot wrote of, and the raid involves some risk, some loss as well as gain. What we can paraphrase is not the poem, just as the obituary is not the life, the belief is not the reality. The name inside the name cannot be named. In its challenging simplicity, Kevin Hart's poetry presents us— beautifully, indelibly—with the human position.

Ariel and Co.

LES MURRAY,
CALLY CONAN-DAVIES

YOU OPEN A MAGAZINE and read. The poems certainly look like poems—written in lines, with some degree of attention to words used and words not used. Yet you can't help feeling the essential art has been given away, the poet too eager to be seen by critics, so the discourse of the poem is nearly indistinguishable from the classroom explanations of an unenthusiastic lecturer. The poems might intrigue the mind but don't touch the body or the emotions. Gone is the subterranean music that leaves a critic drop-jawed and mute. So much of what you see is conceptual art—art that says, "Look at me, I'm art. I dare you to say I am not art. I am approved by my fellow artists. They get me. They know what I'm about."

And there it is. You want to remind people what poetry can do, how it can sing beyond the genius of the sea, but your voice has grown hoarse with such hectoring.

Then one lucky morning you read a great poet. Let's say you take up the *New Selected Poems* of Les Murray, and your thumb finds near the middle of the book a little poem called "Ariel":

Upward, cheeping, on huddling wings,
these small brown mynas have gained
a keener height than their kind ever sustained
but whichever of them falls first
falls to the hawk circling under
who drove them up.
Nothing's free when it is explained.

This too is a work of conceptual art—aimed at the critic, but also at any reader of poetry. And it begins in the great realm of the forgotten common—nature—that world you have to lift your eyes from a smart phone to apprehend. Life and death are at stake. Survival itself is at stake, and beauty and song rolled into gently artful lines. What is "gained" is "sustained," but not too long, and not, of course, "explained," and what "falls first" meets a well-timed line break as it "falls" yet again in space and in our consciousness. The poem is an importance, a small thing with magnitude, like a bird. Your mouth considers other sounds—*gained keener kind*—your eye notes the delayed information about the hawk "who drove them up." And the fuller pleasures of poetry make themselves available. The proper response is gratitude, I suppose, which you can take into your living, breathing, seeing and hearing day, your sensual day, the only day you have.

From its first page, Murray's *New Selected Poems* roars to life with another image of flight—equally violent, equally beautiful—in "The Burning Truck":

It began at dawn with fighter planes:
they came in off the sea and didn't rise,
they leaped the sandbar one and one and one
coming so fast the crockery they shook down
off my kitchen shelves was spinning in the air
when they were gone.

They came in off the sea and drew a wave
of lagging cannon-shells across our roofs.
Windows spat glass, a truck took sudden fire,
out leaped the driver, but the truck ran on,
growing enormous, shambling by our street doors,
coming and coming . . .

Murray is Australia's best known poet, and perhaps he has in mind the Japanese attack on Darwin in World War II. He doesn't say. Nor does he say whose point of view this is, though it seems based on someone's actual memories of an event. The beginning is all movie action in words, and then we have that burning truck, perhaps calling to mind Robert Southwell's "Burning Babe" with its mysticism and religious vision. And this is the core of Les Murray's work: this verbal excitement, this astonishment at the world charged with the grandeur of God. The burning truck keeps rolling, burning and melting, "over the tramlines, past the church, on past / the last lit windows, and then out of the world / with its disciples." One thinks of the visionary leap at the end of Larkin's "High Windows" to that "sun-comprehending glass." The word "disciples" offers scriptural connotations, but perhaps these are secular disciples taking sides in war, or perhaps merely those who will be left fumbling for the story of a great event. What is world or word or being? It's all up for grabs in a poem as exciting as an action film—the sort of performance too few contemporary poets dare to attempt.

Les Murray has been called a poet of rage—at those who bullied him as an overweight child, at class prejudice, which is supposed not to exist in Australia, at an anti-rural, urban, academic elitism that would seem to marginalize him in his own country. But while those emotions are identifiable in the poems, he is much more than they imply. He's a religious poet in the best sense of the word—a poet of verbal incarnations, of deep curiosity and learning. One imagines a large fellow who can move and speak with utmost delicacy and grace, who can invite a loving clumsiness into his lines when it suits him, who loves underdogs as well as signs and wonders.

Even his more editorial poems, where he's presenting ideas about poetry, expand the view. "Religions are poems," he declares in "Poetry and Religion." Huh? That will stop you in your tracks for a while. You see too much evidence of religion as prejudice, religion as motive for murder. But Murray's root meanings prefigure our failings. He's thinking of the *place* of poetry and the *place* of prayer: "Nothing's said till it's dreamed out in words / and nothing's true that figures in words only." If the poem does not, like prayer, open a fissure in the inexpressible, it is a narrower phenomenon than it might be. "Full religion is the large poem in loving repetition. . . ." Now, you might think, you're on shaky ground. Can poems be a form of totalitarianism? Not in Murray's sense: "You can't pray a lie, said Huckleberry Finn; / you can't poe one either."

"An Absolutely Ordinary Rainbow" begins with "a fellow crying in Martin Place. They can't stop him." It's the overspilling force of a very real part of existence:

Some will say, in the years to come, a halo
or force stood around him. There is no such thing.
Some will say they were shocked and would have stopped him
but they will not have been there. The fiercest manhood,
the toughest reserve, the slickest wit among us

trembles with silence, and burns with unexpected
judgements of peace. Some in the concourse scream
who thought themselves happy. Only the smallest children
and such as look out of Paradise come near him
and sit at his feet, with dogs and dusty pigeons.

Ridiculous, says a man near me, and stops
his mouth with his hands, as if it uttered vomit—

and I see a woman, shining, stretch her hand
and shake as she receives the gift of weeping;
as many as follow her also receive it

and many weep for sheer acceptance, and more
refuse to weep for fear of all acceptance,
but the weeping man, like the earth, requires nothing,
the man who weeps ignores us, and cries out
of his writhen face and ordinary body

not words, but grief, not messages, but sorrow,
hard as the earth, sheer, present as the sea—
and when he stops, he simply walks between us
mopping his face with the dignity of one
man who has wept, and now has finished weeping.

Evading believers, he hurries off down Pitt Street.

I was going to end that quote much earlier, but found I couldn't
stop. The poem compelled me. It's the real thing.

Of course Murray is also rambunctiously funny. His earthy
badinage can be found in anthology pieces like "The Quality of
Sprawl" (missing from the present volume) and "The Dream of
Wearing Shorts Forever." There's a wonderful "Homage to the
Launching-place" (bed) and a piquant piece on "The sad surre-
alism of the deaf." These are poems whose company you want
to keep rather than poems that wear out their welcome. They
are challenging in diction and range of reference, sometimes
especially for the non-Australian who has to be brought up to
speed on Strine (as the dialect is affectionately called). The late
Dennis O'Driscoll, interviewing Murray for *The Paris Review*,
noted the poet's "panoptic vision of—and for—Australia." The
interview shows Murray in good form, but he's the same man
you find in the poems: "The only politics I believe in is uncon-
ditional polite welfare. Anybody who needs should have their
needs supplied—and politely. I'm a dissident author; the dead-
liest inertia is to conform with your times." Take *that*, all you

contemporary poets! Zing! "Too much / of poetry is criticism now," he says in "On the Borders." *Amen.*

We've had some large volumes of "Selected Poems" lately from the likes of Heaney and Walcott, and by comparison this one, at under three hundred pages, is a sensible fit in the hand. But it still conveys such a feeling of breadth, so much vitality and fresh air, that you find yourself listing far too many poems to quote. Murray uses measure and rhyme deftly when he wishes to. He writes wonderfully in dialect. He is a master of the narrative mode as well as the lyric and the meditation. He bends grammar with Poundian aplomb when he wants torque to make it real: "I am lived. I am died." He writes with sweet sympathy for animals and can be hard on humans at their worst. And always there is a concern to set the language free and to get it right. In a great sequence of calendar poems filling the middle pages of the book, he asserts, "A poem is an after-life on earth." Les Murray is one of the few poets alive who can make a believer of you.

CONSIDER ANOTHER bird poem:

> We've all heard that thud—
> stunned on the grass,
> breathing hard, drawn close
> to the hollow flight-feather,
> beak cranking, the claw
> scratching at air
> till the neck warps, under
> the sun-struck wall—
> the other side of love.

First published in *The New Criterion* (April 2012), "Wompoo Fruit Dove" announces in its title that it is not an American poem. Cally Conan-Davies is an Australian poet living in America, and among the things she misses about her homeland are the rich inter-layerings of birdlife.* In particular, the Wompoo Fruit Dove is notable for its size and rainbow beauty. The bird's body can grow to be eighteen inches in length, with a wingspan of several feet. If one of these birds hit your window and died, you would notice.

The poem is only nine lines long, seven of them comprising the description of a dying bird set between dashes, so there are two grammatical turns—one at each dash. It's the second turn, however, that deepens the poetry by opening up an unexpected imaginal space as it completes the sentence. The best poems, it would seem, all have at least one such moment, a crack in our expectations that offers us a way into experience beyond the paraphrasable.

So as Americans, if indeed we are Americans, we begin with the estrangement of the title, naming a creature with which we are unfamiliar, and the bluntness of that first line. We think we are reading a poem about a bird hitting a window and dying, which of course means the bird has been fooled by reflections, by images, and has rushed headlong to its death.

Conan-Davies always lets sound lead the eye and ear from line to line, the assonance of "thud" and "stunned"; the off-rhyme of "grass" and "close"; of "feather," "air" and "under"; of "claw" and "wall." Her visual precision, really a lifetime of close observation of the natural world, is brought to bear on the bird: "beak cranking, the claw / scratching the air / till the neck warps . . ." Now it's sharp alliteration we hear, a painful exertion of dying. That word "cranking" was the first big surprise for me—a very particular way of *turning*, or straining to turn, as the move from life to death is a strain to turn into something else. Then that warping neck—the word "warp" is a bent sound to my ear.

---

*I should reveal that Cally Conan-Davies is the pen name of my wife, Chrissy Mason. I choose to write about her here because she is another of my favorite Australian poets, and the poem itself fits well with the work of Les Murray.

When a poet so fully embodies experience in words, we are left to talk about that embodiment in ways that leave merely cerebral intelligence in the dust. This embodiedness is an essentially *poetic* experience.

And then comes the final cranking or shocking turn to "the other side of love." Suddenly the poem has sent us flying into our own mirrored windows. Now we know what the thud meant. It meant that love—everything that had lifted our hearts and made us hope for the future, everything that made us want to dance in ecstasy—has come crashing down in ruins. Or perhaps it means that love is necessarily imaginative, even delusional, a force of both life and death. The poem reveals us to ourselves, refusing to flatter us. We are no better than the deluded bird, chasing images, perhaps images of ourselves, our kind, into oblivion.

The poem's brevity and refusal of sentiment are part of its power. It has the power to stun. The spaces it has opened up reveal life and death, love (which of course rhymes with dove) and the end of love, in a conversation we will never finish.

Voices, Places

Voices, Places

There is no capital of the world, neither here nor anywhere else . . .

—Czesław Miłosz

Question: How is Venice like Idaho?

Answer: Ezra Pound and Ernest Hemingway.

And how are voices like places? They move through us as
we move through them. The voices of great writers guide us
without telling us where we are going—except, of course, to
that most obvious destination of all. We are guided by ambiguity—that's the way literature works. And the way travel works
as well. Travel is a curiosity. We understand it only when we
stop moving, sit still, and begin to listen back.

These are notes from a journey of surprising correspon-
dences, distant rhymes. Voices, places. They begin at startled
dawn and end with an unpacked suitcase, and in between lie
impressions both Mediterranean and Pacific. Impressions are
presences you can't hold on to, like lives.

Bells

We woke each morning to church bells in Nauplion, the beautiful Venetian port in the Peloponnesus and the first capital

of modern Greece. The nearest bells made out a pattern you could dance to:

onetwothreefour
onetwothreefour
onetwothree
onetwothree
onetwothreefour

Weeks later the bells in Venice were more profound, authoritative, gonging beyond the big domes as if to sound out heaven:

God God God God

Everything in Venice had weathered confidence—even the odd face screaming in silent fragments from a wall. Every corner presented another vision of life with its monsters of grace.

Greece had been otherwise, so many of its churches, chapels, and monasteries in remote, unpopulated places. In Mani, the long rough peninsula between snowy Taygetus and the Ionian Sea, the churches used to be left open—no longer possible with the increase in tourism, vandalism, and theft. At one gorgeous little church the bell hung outside in an olive tree. It was off a footpath to the spit of land called *Tigani*, or frying pan. The anonymous frescoes inside were finely modeled and undamaged. The saints I have forgotten now, but not the silence of the thorny and rocky land, the bell and the calm sea.

That bell was such a small clear voice.

There are voices that cut through the detritus of the world, some of them without sound, voices seemingly inside the dome of the mind. These are voices we follow all our lives, too many of them even to name. Among the voices I hear are two Americans with strained relations to their native country, two writers whose stock has fallen, at least in some circles. It is necessary to re-read writers whose stock has fallen.

Let us follow them a while. There is no path, but there are footsteps, dark as ink. They will not lead in a straight line, but circle back upon themselves like readings of a poem. There is a memory of bells—goat bells, church bells—weathering in the years. Follow the echoes.

Ez

What were his earliest memories? What did he know at the end, when they took him to the hospital in Venice? What does dementia erase?

We were in Idaho, driving west on Highway 20 past the Craters of the Moon. We stopped so my wife could photograph the eerie light, the sage against black volcanic buttes and canyons and shrouding clouds. I picked up pieces of pumice like sharp lumps of charred breath.

In magic hours traveling in place means traveling in time, as if a door opens and you see through to the eternal presence. I had premonitions all along that road, notions of connection.

On the map I saw Hailey, Idaho, just ahead. Pound was born there. And Hemingway shot himself just up the road in Ketchum. In Venice not two weeks earlier we had seen Pound's grave. Maybe this would round out the journey in some way, give it shape. Maybe Venice and Idaho were not so far apart.

When we turned north off Highway 20 it was into another state. The wealth of outsiders and ski resort people came into view with the big ranches, the white fences, the bike paths. The bare hills were immaculate.

In Hailey we saw the small white clapboard house at 314 Second Avenue where Ezra Pound was born, now a center for the arts with a barn-like classroom building behind.

It had rained hard that morning, and the blossoming crabapple tree in the front yard had black boughs. Pound was only eighteen months old when his mother, Isabel, who disliked living in Hailey, took him back east to be near her family. Could he have remembered those petals on a wet black bough when, in the grips of Imagist theories in 1913, he whittled a longer poem down to two now-famous lines?

The apparition   of these faces   in the crowd   :
Petals   on a wet, black   bough   .

Could he have remembered the smell of the limber pine on the north side of the house? His father, Homer, had come to Hailey by presidential appointment as a Registrar of Mines. What sort of Yankee talk would the baby have heard on those front steps? What drove his mother away? Were the hills so unbeautiful to her? Were the people too rough?

Pound always had a measure of contempt for America. In "To Whistler, American," he had written in 1912:

You had your searches, your uncertainties,
And this is good to know—for us, I mean,
Who bear the brunt of our America
And try to wrench her impulse into art.

You were not always sure, not always set
To hiding night or tuning "symphonies";
Had not one style from birth, but tried and pried
And stretched and tampered with the media.

You and Abe Lincoln from that mass of dolts
Show us there's chance at least of winning through.

Long before I understood much of his poetry, Pound's irascible character, discovered in paperback anthologies, beguiled and fascinated. The way he tampered with his medium, the way he used the old to fashion something new, made a believer of me. I believed in literature, the great revivifying fountain of stories and poems that existed somewhere far away, I thought, from the American West.

No, he can't have remembered Hailey, Idaho. His family moved back to Pennsylvania and Homer got a job at the Philadelphia Mint. Pound grew up relatively privileged, able to feed his romanticism. He kept trying to improve America with his ideas, just as he tried to improve literature with one theory after another. Then he tried to improve England and France. Eventually it looked as though Italy had been sufficiently improved, so he went there to live among the fascists.

He said hateful things. Archibald MacLeish reported to Ernest Hemingway during World War II that their friend was making anti-Semitic radio broadcasts in Rome. Hemingway wrote back from Cuba that Ezra was clearly crazy.

But was he crazy or was he merely capable of saying truly hateful things about Jews? Doctors diagnosed him as schizophrenic. Others privately felt he was a raging narcissist. Still others that his monomania for fixing things was detached from any ability to live in the real world.

Yet he could write in the *Pisan Cantos*, "Pull down thy vanity, / I say pull down." Can such a voice be dismissed simply because it rose from a man of error?

Well, *yes*. Pound can drive you nuts.

Hem

In Ketchum the tourist information office is also a Starbucks. We stood with our lattes and talked to a gentle fellow named Bill who liked his life in Idaho very much and told us about the summer symphony. The town sounded a bit like Aspen with less bulk and ostentation. The homes of the very rich and the clubbiness of the Sun Valley Lodge were hard to take, but otherwise it looked like a town with real life in it.

Bill had been allowed inside the house where Hemingway shot himself in 1961. The family had closed it up and left it as it was. Hermetically sealed. We drove near the river and looked in past the shut gate. A sad thing, secret beyond the trees and scrub and the straggly blossoms. A house where he would have heard the river roaring with life night and day.

Up the Sun Valley Road a bust of Ernest Hemingway stares off toward the hills. An inscription, a lively stream. And just a short way up Highway 75 there lay the grave, and Mary's grave next to him, and on the other side the grave of his son John Hadley Nicanor.

Ernest Hemingway's slab was covered with coins and an admirer had left a half-empty bottle of absinthe.

I am not first of all thinking of the bluster, the machismo, the sorry image of the fat braggart. I am thinking of lovely, lovely sentences, superb stories—virtually all of the early work from *In Our Time* to *For Whom the Bell Tolls*, or at least the best parts of it, and even some of the later work like *A Moveable Feast*. Re-reading *The Sun Also Rises*, I was shocked by the anti-Semitism. Is it Hem's or is it his characters', and how can you tell? How can such shit get mixed in with such beauty? His interview with *The Paris Review* reveals deep modesty and vocation: "The further you go in writing the more alone you are." You keep company with the dead in so many ways.

Re-reading his best stories, I get not only sharp impressions of the physical world, but also his sensitivity to the woundedness of others. And what superb *writing*. Before it became mannered and manly. What feeling. How much it had meant to me, growing up in the West when it seemed a relatively empty and unlettered place. How much it had meant to read "The Big Two-Hearted River" and find an image of life that could have been my own, though I knew little of his war experience. Hemingway led me to other writers: Maupassant, Chekhov, Turgenev, Tolstoy, Twain, and even through odd associations his friend Ezra Pound.

He met Pound in Paris. In March 1922 he wrote to Sherwood Anderson (the misspellings are part of the charm), "I've been teaching Pound to box wit little success. He habitually leads wit his chin and has the general grace of the crayfish or crawfish." The early letters are full of fresh spirit. 1922 was the year of Joyce's *Ulysses* and Eliot's "The Waste Land," which appeared in the *Dial* in November. Hemingway wrote to Pound,

> I still think you are the only living poet altho. I am glad to read Herr Elliot's adventure away from impeccability. If Herr Elliot would strangle his sick wife, bugger the brain specialist and rob the bank he might write an even better poem.
>
> The above is facetious.

And here they were, connected by a short drive between Hailey and Ketchum. Connected also by Venice.

Hemingway thought his Venetian novel, *Across the River and Into the Trees*, published in 1950, one of his most sophisticated experiments. Critics panned it. John O'Hara wrote wittily about it in *The New York Times Book Review*, allowing for some of the mockery the book received but still admiring the author's skill.

The book tells of fifty-year-old Colonel Cantwell, who is infatuated with an eighteen-year-old girl, Renatta—one of Hemingway's fantasy women, not one of his sharply drawn characters like Pilar or Brett Ashley. It was partly the novel's structure that put critics off—the long flashback of a dying man—partly the feeling that his prose had become self-imitative. The reviews got under his skin. Even the later success of *The Old Man and the Sea* (as nearly perfect as anything he wrote) and the Nobel Prize did not help him deal with his personal demons. The son of a suicide, he committed suicide himself in 1961.

Hemingway's body was taken to the coroner in Hailey, then back up to Ketchum for burial. The road like a birthcord or deathcord or musical chord connecting two American writers, both of them deeply flawed believers in the importance of literature, leaving their scattered legacies.

And we were really there, having been in Venice at the grave of Ezra Pound exactly two weeks earlier. There in the rain, the smell of wet leaves and pine cones and mown grass. Hemingway's son John, his child by his first wife, Hadley, lay next to his father. John had made his own sort of nobility, living with his father's legacy and dying in that town.

The grandchildren are still around, Bill told us. Mariel has made a film about the family disease. The suicides.

Reading and Moving

When we drove away, north on Highway 75, we passed the grave again. My wife said out the car window, "Goodbye, Hemingway! Thank you for everything. Thank you, thank you, thank you." He had been such a helpful model for her students in Australia. When she needed to teach the writing of good sentences, she could tell them to walk in his footprints.

It was a lovely image. We walk in the footprints of the great writers. When we move through the world their lines and sentences continue to guide us, as if they looked on and helped. Recently I read Richard Holmes's book, *Footsteps*, in which biography takes on the obsessions of travel and memoir, the author pursuing such figures as Robert Louis Stevenson, Mary Wollstonecraft, Percy Bysshe Shelley, and Gérard de Nerval through the very places in which they had lived and traveled.

Holmes pursued the lives of his subjects, testing ambiguous evidence. With Pound and Hemingway it was more their words, their best lines and sentences, I wanted to follow. Still, how haunting it was to touch places they had touched—the Hemingway house in Key West, for example, with its austere writing room and garden full of cats. And the narrow street of Pound's final Venice digs, the plaque above the door. And the wet black boughs of his birthplace.

It moves me to imagine them as people—vitally flawed, cornered by the very lives they had created. Perhaps Pound had no memory of the white clapboard house, the lilacs in the yard, the blossoming crab. But perhaps the bare hills had cast a permanent light on his consciousness, like the background of a Renaissance painting. Perhaps they were why he thought America worth saving and tried so hard to keep us from entering the war.

Of course he was wrong. But not all of the reasons he was wrong were wrong. He hated war, and thought our economics perpetuated such conflicts, and he certainly had a point about that. He was not the only intellectual to espouse fascism or spout anti-Semitic drivel. Looking back on his life, he told Allen Ginsberg he had made a terrible mistake. And he told Donald Hall in 1960, "You—find me—in fragments."

Still, on his release from St. Elizabeth's and his return to Italy, what did he do? He gave a fascist salute. He said, ". . . all America is an insane asylum."

Sometimes I sympathize with him on that latter score. Driving the freeways in America, one only has the corporate side of the country to admire—the malls and chain restaurants—and the nation seems a soulless failure nearly everywhere you look. An economic dynamo, but alienating, adolescent, amnesiac.

That was why this journey on the back roads, the smaller highways, had been so reinvigorating, reminding me that my country could be a beautiful place, despite the corporate ownership of our politics, our troglodytic gun laws, our crazy failure to fund education and healthcare, our fundamentalist Christians, our packed prisons and drone warfare.

What did Pound remember when they took him to the hospital in Venice? Did he remember the lush green summers in Pennsylvania? Proposing to Hilda Doolittle and having her father reject the marriage? Standing as best man at Yeats's wedding, his own wedding to Dorothy Shakespear, daughter of Yeats's lover, or falling in love with Olga Rudge, the American violinist? Did he remember his daughter Mary (by Olga) or his son Omar (from Dorothy's affair with another man), or how in 1926 it was his friend Ernest Hemingway who drove Dorothy to the hospital to give birth? Walking most of 450 miles north out of Rome to stay ahead of the Allied invasion? The cage at Pisa? A drive through upstate New York with James Laughlin—how they stopped at a Howard Johnson's restaurant to eat?

Did he remember the blossoming crab in the front yard of the house in Hailey, Idaho? Petals on a wet black bough?

What are the images imprinted on a brain that make a poet? What are the images that make a madman or a traitor?

The plaque on the house in Hailey reads:

BIRTHPLACE

OF

EZRA POUND

THE POET

OCTOBER 30, 1885

"I HAVE BEATEN OUT MY EXILE"

Pound beat time and time beat Pound right into the ground. Some unkillable poems have outlived him, and some feisty remarks that will stick in the craw of literature.

Isola di San Michele

The *vaporetto* crossed quickly to the cemetery island, and we stepped into a walled garden of birdsong and grief. In addition to Pound's grave, we wanted to find Brodsky and Stravinsky.

First we found the graves of children, the weeping angels.

In the section of new burials where we looked for Brodsky's grave, a splendid gull alighted on a headstone and began squawking. He was beautiful, so white and healthy looking, and he squawked *Life! Life you fools! Life!* He was a poet.

The rosebush and flowers on Brodsky's pristine plot with its elegant stone. *LETUM NON OMNIA FINIT*—death does not end it all.

Pound's overgrown grave lay next to the grave of Olga Rudge. I left a token stone above the P.

Elsewhere in Venice you see graffiti from an organization calling itself CasaPound—neo-fascists of some sort. Their use of his name in this new time of crisis is obscene. It has deeply upset his daughter, Mary. Of course they wouldn't care who they upset. The dead have no control over what is made about them, what is said about them. And the living have no way of knowing whether what they make or say is the truth.

People will be arguing about his fascism for years, and some will be wondering how he could be the same man who spent so much of his life helping others, urging them on, getting them published. Those who love difficulty will usually cite portions of the *Cantos* or "Homage to Sextus Propertius" or "Mauberley" for the best of Ezra Pound, but I can't help loving simpler poems, such as "Alba":

> As cool as the pale wet leaves
> > of lily-of-the-valley
> She lay down beside me in the dawn.

Tactile quietude, the words inhabited bodily—I can learn from that, and from garrulous poems like "The Garret":

> Come, let us pity those who are better off than we are.
> Come, my friend, and remember
> > that the rich have butlers and no friends,
> And we have friends and no butlers.
> Come, let us pity the married and the unmarried.

> Dawn enters with little feet
> > like a gilded Pavlova,
> And I am near my desire.
> Nor has life in it aught better
> Than this hour of clear coolness,
> > the hour of waking together.

The island cemetery of Venice is among other things a shrine to the arts. Part of its beauty is the pursuit of beauty, an atmosphere enhanced by the heavy breath of extinction. So we walked among the dead hearing voices, footsteps, music.

Diaghilev's grave was covered with ballet slippers. On Stravinsky's grave someone had left a heart-shaped stone, but rain had washed it aside.

In a nearby corner of the cemetery leaned an unexpected stone:

ASPASIA
WIDOW OF
H. M.
ALEXANDER I
KING OF THE HELLENES
1898–1972

We were, in fact, journeying home from an extended sojourn in crisis-stricken Greece, and somehow this marker moved me back to that small bell in the olive tree.

That small clear voice in the boughs.

Footsteps

For a while I tried putting photographs side by side: the Grand Tetons next to the domes of Venice, the lion of St. Mark's next to bison fording a Wyoming river. These things were only connected, perhaps, by the desire to connect them, the journey through time and space. How is Venice like Idaho? Two troubled writers, the visible fact of their graves. The story linking these things is part of the meaning of place. Telling the story voice-maps the land, locating us with others who have been there before.

I think of Venice grandly melting on its canals, the intensity of color in those intricate oil paintings, the way that singular city dissolves the difference between a museum and a life.

Petals on a wet black bough in Idaho, the plaque on white clapboards there. The names carved in stone in the island cemetery: Ezra and Olga, Joseph, Igor, Aspasia . . . *Life!* cries the gull strutting on a grave. *Life!*

The dancing bells of Greece. The small clear voice in the olive tree.

Mary Hemingway saw her husband lingering about the gun case at their home in Ketchum and was worried. In his last letter from the hospital in Rochester, Minnesota, Hemingway sounded chipper and eager to live and be healthy again. Something happened. Something made it all go wrong.

What did Pound remember when they took him to the hospital in Venice? What did Hemingway mean by shooting himself in the entryway to that house? The door is closed and locked, the house shrouded and shut away almost as he left it.

And there are sentences so full of the ecstatic grief of physical sensation that I will never stop admiring them. Light on a river. The color of leaves in the fall. The way a fish fights for life. The solitary body, the burned forest, the unstated wound, the estrangements of men and women. The suicide of an Indian man in a remote Michigan camp. The way lake water feels to a boy swirling his hand in it. The menacing talk of killers ordering food in a diner. The dry white stones of a riverbed. The pine-needled floor of a forest.

We have arrived in Oregon for the summer. Light in the Sitka spruces, the Pacific rising and falling below like great lungs of the earth. The end of the open road. The daily presence of life and death on the shore.

To Humanize the "Inhumanist"

ROBINSON JEFFERS

In 1932, when Robinson Jeffers appeared on the cover of *Time* magazine, looking chiseled as a movie star, he was the most famous poet in America. His reputation has waned, yet a few poets and devoted scholars have kept his poems in print, periodically arguing for Jeffers' importance, and his face has more recently appeared on a postage stamp. Perhaps now, with the publication of the third and final volume of his letters and a short biography by their editor, James Karman, the time has come to bring Jeffers back to a wide readership. The letters detail his life in its dailiness with surprising outbursts of drama, while Karman's biography places Jeffers in the larger context of literary history. Taken together, they are very nearly the major, full-length study Jeffers really deserves.

The peer of modern poets like Eliot, Frost, Moore, and Stevens, Jeffers (1887–1962) was unusual in the ambitious range of his narrative and dramatic poetry as well as his lyrics. Unlike Eliot and other modernists, he avoided dense, allusive structures, trusting story and direct emotion to do the work.

Karman argues that California, the mixed-race heroine of Jeffers' early narrative, "Roan Stallion," resembles "Pasiphaë, the woman in Greek mythology who loved a bull." But Jeffers probes her psychology like a novelist. She's torn between love of the stallion's wild energy, "the savage and exultant strength of the world," and "some obscure human fidelity." Her conflict ends in shocking tragedy. Violence erupts in most of Jeffers' longer works, which, like some biblical stories and Greek myths, include incest and parricide. But there is also a larger vision of "the sublime beauty and supreme indifference of nature." He denied his critics' charge of pessimism, writing in 1943 to a friend, "Civilizations rise and fall, ours has risen and will fall, so will others in the future—[To say so] is no more pessimistic than to say men are born and will die." To Jeffers our animal nature should not be ignored. In a late poem he even imagines being eaten by a vulture: "What a sublime end of one's body, what an enskyment; what a life after death."

This philosophy, which Jeffers called "Inhumanism," has turned some squeamish readers away. Horace Gregory noticed it as early as 1955, commenting in "Poet Without Critics" that Jeffers' poems were "at once too directly spoken and, beneath their surfaces, too deeply felt and too complex" to be fodder for the typical university classroom. Jeffers needs defenders, and Karman is one of the most loyal of them, not only in the biography, but also in allowing Jeffers and his wife, Una, to be heard in their letters. These books draw us back again to the poems, which constitute a powerful antidote to our narcissistic culture. "As for us," Jeffers wrote in "Carmel Point," "We must uncenter our minds from ourselves; / We must unhumanize our views a little. . . ." He is a prophet of the human position within nature—not superior to it or above it but "confident / As the rock and ocean that we were made from."

You can read the three volumes of the letters almost as acts of a play, each with a central set of problems and revelations. Volume One is a story of beginnings.

John Robinson Jeffers was born in Allegheny, Pennsylvania. His father, William Hamilton Jeffers, was a Presbyterian minister and professor of church history and literature as well as eight ancient languages. The biography tells us little about Jeffers' mother, Annie Tuttle, but the letters suggest her supportive, open spirit. From his father love came sternly: "When I was nine years old," Jeffers wrote in 1953, "my father began to slap Latin into me, literally, with his hands; and when I was eleven he put me in a boarding-school in Switzerland—a new one every year for four years—Vevey, Lausanne, Geneva, Zurich. Then he brought me home and put me in college as a sophomore." By then "home" was Highland Park, California, where the family moved in 1903. He graduated from Occidental College in 1905 at age eighteen, already a publishing poet, as highly educated as any writer of his generation. After a semester at the University of Zurich he returned to the States and tried, as he put it, "three years in medical school—not knowing what else to do; and then drifted into mere drunken idleness."

By that time Jeffers had met his future wife, Una Call Kuster, in a German literature class at the University of Southern California. Una's husband, Teddie, was a well-known attorney, musician, and supporter of the arts. Her love affair with Robin (as he was familiarly known) became a public scandal, spilling into the *Los Angeles Times* in 1912. Teddie demanded that his wife go abroad for a period of separation, but Robin already felt transformed, telling Una, ". . . you are integrating my personality." He would later write, "My nature is cold and undiscriminating; she excited and focused it, gave it eyes and nerves and sympathies."

The Collected Letters of Robinson Jeffers is subtitled "With Selected Letters of Una Jeffers," but for many pages you might think the titles should be reversed. Jeffers was a fitful correspondent, often complaining of "my idiot inability to answer a letter." Once the newly-married couple established their household in Carmel, California, in 1914, Una took over much of the correspondence. The poet was free to spend his mornings writing verse, his afternoons apprenticing to a stonemason, building Tor House, their idiosyncratic home above the sea. But in the years of courtship and separation before their marriage we find Jeffers writing ardent love letters, and Una responding with equal fervor. She also wrote witheringly honest letters to Teddie:

> I *knew* it was normal, my passion—I knew it was right it should be satisfied and I felt I was being cheated.—If after a while I was to blame for many things—that is another matter—I have been talking about this in its incipiency. I came to feel you were not my equal sexually. . . .

The Jeffers marriage began in scandal and grief—their first child, a daughter, only lived a day—but was founded on mutual esteem as well as sexual attraction. Despite two later love affairs on Jeffers' part, he and Una remained devoted to each other the rest of their lives. They also maintained friendship with Teddie, who eventually built a house nearby and founded a professional theater in the town.

Rhythms of the sea and building with stone transformed the poet. "As Jeffers worked on Tor House," Karman writes, "the doors of perception—the fullness of his own poetic consciousness—opened, and the world suddenly (over the course of a summer) became timeless and transparent." He was writing in long tidal lines new narratives comparable to the fiction of D. H. Lawrence. He also wrote visionary lyrics like "To the Stone Cutters" and "Continent's End," as well as penetrating later poems like "Love the Wild Swan":

> Does it matter whether you hate your . . . self? At least
> Love your eyes that can see, your mind that can
> Hear the music, the thunder of the wings. Love the wild swan.

Though his poems are often about what he called "falling in love outward," it's hard to imagine a more domestically-inclined writer. He seldom left work in the family compound, and in the evenings read novels by lamplight to his twin sons, Garth and Donnan, born in 1916.

Volume Two of the letters reveals a more shocking personal conflict. In the 1930s, at the height of his fame, he was lured to Taos, New Mexico, by the meddlesome patroness and collector of artists Mabel Dodge Luhan. Her memoir, *Lorenzo in Taos* (1932), was "composed as a long letter to Jeffers" in which she claimed to have willed D.H. Lawrence to come to her. She was now trying the same with Jeffers. In July 1938, feeling blocked as a writer, and perhaps hemmed in by Una's powerful personality, Jeffers fell in love with another of Mabel's guests, Hildegarde Donaldson. Mabel had encouraged the affair, then pretended indifference to it all. "But now," she recalls in an unpublished manuscript Karman quotes in his footnotes to the letters, "Una's instinct smouldering before, was somehow thoroughly aroused. She began to watch like a crouching tigress." One night Robin came running from the guest house to announce, "Una's shot herself . . . come . . . come."

Mabel found Hildegarde unconscious at the foot of the staircase, having knocked her head against a beam when the pistol shot startled her, and Una upstairs bleeding in a bathtub: "Her face was like that of a maenad. When she saw me she ground out: 'Did she smash her head? Is she dead? I hope so. I'm dying, but I'll meet her in hell.'"

Una survived the suicide attempt, claiming it was an accident, and a chastened Robin brought his family home to Carmel. Letters to Hildegarde ended soon after, and in Volume Three we learn the pitiful denouement. Mabel finds a devastated Hildegarde in 1946 "with white hair, hollow cheeks, missing teeth, twisted fingers, colorless skin, and dull, dead-looking eyes," gasping, "Mabel—I think—Una—put—a—spell on me." Jeffers had just published his great version of Euripides' tragedy *Medea*, and Luhan used the opportunity to turn Una into her own version of the Black Sea witch.

Jeffers never sought fame—a late poem imagines "a man at the gate to meet visitors, / Saying 'Jeffers is not at home. Jeffers has gone to Llasa. / Jeffers is buying camels in Urga'"—but the human tide caught up with him. California's population tripled in his lifetime and the property boom ate up the last open spaces around Tor House. His anti-interventionist stance during World War II, his consistent vision of America "heavily thickening into empire," and the outrage he expressed in *The Double Axe and Other Poems* (1948), a volume published with a cautious disclaimer by Random House, caused many critics to turn away. He remained paradoxically popular: his *Medea*, especially in performances around the world by Judith Anderson, won rapturous acclaim. A later televised version reached more than two million viewers, and the play remains one of the best modern verse dramas we have. Other works were more controversial. A drama based on his *Dear Judas* met with accusations of blasphemy. Jeffers took it all in stride, indifferent to both praise and condemnation.

Volume Three shows Jeffers himself corresponding more after Una's death, dealing with theater business, translations of his works, his "fans," critics and friends, so we hear more of his kind and patient and grieving voice. The last book he published, *Hungerfield and Other Poems* (1954), contains a lurid narrative sandwiched between heartbreaking verses for Una. An equally beautiful tribute to her can be found in the posthumous *Selected Poetry of Robinson Jeffers* edited by Tim Hunt (2001):

> It nearly cancels my fear of death, my dearest said,
> When I think of cremation. To rot in the earth
> Is a loathsome end, but to roar up in flame—besides, I am used to it,
> I have flamed with love or fury so often in my life,
> No wonder my body is tired, no wonder it is dying.
> We had great joy of my body. Scatter the ashes.

Robin and Una Jeffers were an extraordinary literary couple, and their letters, by showing us the marriage and his role as husband, father, and grandfather, humanize the Inhumanist. Both emerge as vital figures in these books. Karman's biography will help new readers understand Jeffers' importance, while leaving room for a full-length life in the future. In our trivializing time, the great poet of California remains one of the profound visionaries we need most to hear.

Belle Turnbull's
Western Narrative

How far have we come to feel the shade of this tree?
—Thomas Hornsby Ferril

Belle Turnbull's 1940 "novel in verse," *Goldboat*, is like so many significant poems, an eccentricity. First, it's the work of a poet few of our contemporaries will have read, a woman whose writing received some attention in her lifetime (1881–1970), but has since gone out of print and suffered neglect. She was regional, and her region—Colorado—was rarely perceived as the stuff of important literature, even in the cases of Willa Cather, Wallace Stegner, and others. Turnbull published relatively little—three collections of verse and one prose novel—so she didn't arouse attention through sheer industrious bulk, as some American poets are wont to do. Furthermore, while Turnbull's accomplishment is genuine, some aspects of her work have dated, and this seems especially true of *Goldboat*, with its clumsy representations of racial and sexual relations. But despite such reservations, the book deserves attention for several reasons. First, it is an example of populist modernism, a literary strain including the likes of Carl Sandburg, Robinson Jeffers, and prose writers like John Dos Passos. Turnbull's verse novel uses not only skillful and charged blank verse, but also more fragmentary forms: notations, telegrams, business reports and the like. While it tells a very traditional tale—the plot is more like a short story from *The Saturday Evening Post* than an experimental novel—its modernist techniques complicate and enrich the verse. Turnbull's narrative can also be seen in the context of other long poems from the American West, including works by Thomas McGrath, Edward Dorn, W. S. Merwin, Gary Snyder, and others—verse that incorporates a new mythos and a new geography, as well as an extension of poetry's most ancient storytelling functions.

The narrative poem, especially the "longer narrative," is a sometimes popular curiosity. On the one hand, we have the epic tradition from *Gilgamesh* to *Paradise Lost*, while on the other we have fully religious narratives like the Mahabharata and the Bible. These works use verse to tell stories or pause to give us moments of lyric illumination. Until modern times, few readers ever questioned the viability of verse as a storytelling medium. Tennyson and Longfellow excelled at both lyrics and narratives without ever feeling they were betraying some essential aspect of their art. Yet even in their time, the advent of the novel and more easily available books put poets on notice: their ancient role as storytellers would not last forever. Poe had gone so far as to declare long poems entirely contradictory: "I need scarcely observe that a poem deserves its title only inasmuch as it excites, by elevating the soul. The value of the poem is the ratio of this elevating excitement. But all excitements are, through a psychal necessity, transient. That degree of excitement which would entitle a poem to be so called at all, cannot be sustained through a composition of any great length. At the lapse of half an hour, at the very utmost, it flags— fails—a revulsion ensues—and then the poem is, in effect, and in fact, no longer such."

By the twentieth century, modernism seemed to have blown narrative poetry out of the water. In our own time, quite a few poets and critics, including arbiters of taste like Helen Vendler, have declared their dislike of narrative. And one can see the point. Contemporary American verse too often comprises affectless personal narratives that make the art feel unexciting or irrelevant to readers. Furthermore, when poets completely misunderstand the nearly universal practice called "free verse," writing banal expositional prose stacked up in listless lines and expecting readers to come running—well, readers have good reason not to.

Yet modernism did not really kill fictional narratives in verse. Robinson and Frost wrote them. Jeffers wrote them. Anthony Hecht and Louis Simpson wrote them, and in my own generation the list of writers of verse narratives is very long. Novels in verse are now quite common, no more endangered than novels in prose. The question is, what makes a good *novel* in verse? How are stories most imaginatively rendered? When is verse most skillfully and compellingly used, and when is the poet merely typing in lines without knowing what he or she really ought to be doing?

Belle Turnbull knew exactly what she was doing. She had the skill and the delight in possibilities to make *Goldboat* an example worth study. While I don't think it is a great poem or a great example of the verse novel, I also cannot dismiss it. *Goldboat* is a milestone in the literature of Colorado, and an experiment that writers can learn from. I'm glad I read it only after I had published my own verse novel, *Ludlow*, because if I had known Turnbull's book I might have been tempted to borrow some of its techniques. As it is, our two eccentric efforts can coexist without disturbing each other in the least.

I've written elsewhere that stories are forms, no less than sonnets and villanelles are forms. The paraphrasable part of Turnbull's story is promising. A young mining engineer, John

Dorn,* arrives in the town of Rockinghorse (perhaps a thinly disguised Breckenridge, Colorado), to build a goldboat for a dredging operation. Goldboats were usually floated on man-made ponds as they dug into the adjacent hillsides, moving loam and peat and shale till they got down to the gold ore at bedrock. Disused dredging ponds are still visible in Colorado mountain towns like Leadville. Dorn's work in the bedrock economy of Colorado—mining—positions him between heroic and antiheroic roles. His boss, and the father of his betrothed, Alicia, is a demanding investor on the verge of bankruptcy, and Dorn encounters in the town a more freedom-loving if impoverished people. Clearly he will have to make a choice between rapaciousness and love. The choice he makes is no surprise, and perhaps that is one weakness in Turnbull's book. Her characters lack shadings and complexities.

Still, from the first pages her writing is often vigorous:

Over the Great Divide unrolls the highway
And cars go wagging their tails among the thunders,
Range to range stitching, weather to weather.
In half a day you can hem the watershed
And rush on the prairie or race on the desert again
Unaware of the minute clues of legend,
The featherstitching of roads that thread the meadows,
Follow the gulches, follow the mountain pattern.

One might object to the sewing metaphor for landscape—certainly not as fresh as Elizabeth Bishop's comparison of a fish's skin to wallpaper—but from the opening stanza Turnbull's blank verse rhythms are strong and active:

There wasn't any widgeon or any rocksnake
When young John Dorn came seething into the district

*The name is a funny coincidence, since one of Colorado's narrative poets, the author of *Gunslinger* (1968), was Edward Dorn.

Easing the tires of his palpitant new roadster
Along the corduroy through the Goose Pasture,
With his negro cook adrift and undone in the tonneau
And a goldscale riding hard on her jellied bosom.

The "negro cook," whose name is Thedus, proves both a Hollywood stereotype, a sort of Butterfly McQueen complete with dialect shuffling, and one of the book's more important characters, equipped with a fortuneteller's mystical intuition. Compare her to the adherents of obeah in Jean Rhys's novel, *Wide Sargasso Sea*, and you'll see she's a thinly imagined character:

'UH-uh,' she moaned, 'wasn' yo maw made me
Swear on huh dyin bed to follow yo courses
I suah would bandon you now. An her that's comin,'
Her eyes were baleful, 'I done run the cahds on huh,
Queen of spades an a curse, and Thedus slavin
Under huh lil high heels.'

Luckily this stage vernacular does not go on for long. "Her that's comin" is Alicia, Dorn's beloved—another character so lightly sketched as to be barely visible. The third woman in the story is wonderfully named, Leafy Buffin, the freedom-loving mountain girl we get to know mainly by her attractively willful absence. Thedus is more interesting than either of the white girls:

Thedus wasn't paddling the lodge that evening.
She sat pressed into a corner of her bedplace
In a strongly resinous welter of woodwaste and sawdust
And told the beads of a negro's infinite loneliness
And bonedeep surety of outrageous future.
Lost in a bleak unmellowed white man's country
She stared down the candleray.

Thedus also has her cards, her fortune-telling and magic, which come in handy at the book's climactic moment of decision. Like a seer out of Greek or Roman epic, she tells Dorn that he has a choice: "I see a gole gate / An I see a hawny gate." Not ivory, but gates of gold and horn—to reach his true love, Dorn must pass through the latter.

Turnbull's love story and her protagonist's choice between two women mirrors the economic plot, which is more precisely and satisfyingly dramatized. Not only is her businessman villain more vitally alive than most other characters, but Dorn's struggle, his actual work and the hardships it entails, offers the best writing in the book. Turnbull excels as a poet of work and action. Her first departure from blank verse is in Dorn's report to his boss:

> . . . Old volcanic mountains,
> Eruptive sheets of porphyry
> . . . Communication of values
> . . . Drift of the ice age,
> Fifty glaciers grinding
> . . . Breaking down of fissures
> Where the gold was molten
> . . . Rich float on the benches,
> Washed along the waters
> . . . Light auriferous gravel,
> Loam of the gulches
> . . . Fine gold on the low bars,
> Coarse gold in the nuggets
> . . . Thirty million dollars
> Scarped from the surface
> When the place was booming . . .

In the literature of the American West the desert landscape can seem more alive than the people. Turnbull takes full advantage of alternative formats for versification, from angry telegraph dialogues between Dorn and his boss to a driller's notes and an insidious "Report to Stockholders." Imagine a minimalist version of Paul Thomas Anderson's film *There Will Be Blood*, in which ruthless commerce battles with fraudulent religion. *Goldboat* does not have so broad a canvas or so dark a vision of America, which is one reason why it feels too restrained and minor a work. Still, Turnbull understands the world of kited stocks as well as the work of geologists, diggers, and watchmen. Her poem reminds us of the soulless greed that has erased so much of value in American culture and left its detritus everywhere in our land.

In my favorite parts of *Goldboat*, language itself breaks down and punctuation vanishes. This happens when Dorn feels his first romantic confusion, and again when he's in the midst of important action, trying to save everything he has built:

The guiderope   there, under your hand   now
Feel for the plank   Jesus what an angle
Down into the dark   claw down   down
Maybe next step your foot'll be in water
What's that noise ahead   like wood chattering
Onto wood   why that might be the plank
Hitting against the housing   busted loose
Some chance then

The writing responds to pressure and urgency, as it often should in prose fiction. But a longer narrative poem is not just a string of well-written moments. It has to fill the psychological space of its characters and its dramas, and its lyricism needs to rise above the story on occasion, lifting us to some place we could not find by other means. Readers may disagree about whether Turnbull's restraint is too limiting, whether her story needed just a bit more spark and wildness.

TURNBULL WAS BORN in New York State, and moved with her family to Colorado Springs at the age of nine. She worked as a school teacher, retiring first to Frisco, then to Breckenridge, both mountain towns, in the late 1930s. Clearly she loved the mountains and knew them well. We can also see this in her 1957 collection of lyrics, *The Tenmile Range*, with its sonnets and ballad-like narratives. She would have made a fine poet laureate for the state, I think, and was a much better writer than our first four laureates: Alice Polk Hill (who served from 1919 to 1921), Nellie Burget Miller (1923–52), Margaret Clyde Robertson (1952–54), and Milford E. Shields (1954–75). I mention these names partly to put her in the literary context of Colorado, but also because I want to compare her, briefly, to our fifth poet laureate, Thomas Hornsby Ferril (who served from 1979 to his death in 1988). Like Turnbull, Ferril was a notable poet who has yet to be sufficiently recognized for substantial accomplishments. He was sixteen years younger than Turnbull, but their similarities link them as important twentieth-century Colorado writers. They were both poets of a populist-modernist tradition, masters of a Frostian blank verse as well as other forms, adept as sonneteers, and as attuned to the Rocky Mountain landscape as Frost was to his adopted New England.

As I read Turnbull, I find a handful of her lyrics very fine, and her novel in verse has moments of vivid imagination and power, but in the best poetry the full sweep and anarchy of imagination feel barely contained, and I do think Turnbull's imagination is sometimes too subdued. Ferril was a more freewheeling poet by any measure, yet he never wrote a novel in verse. So the fact of *Goldboat*, the example of it as a book, a polyphonic narrative of nearly eighty pages, is in itself remarkable. Oddly enough, I wish the poem were longer. I wish there were scenes that opened up the chaos and grandeur of her characters' lives, allowing us to feel more of Leafy and Alicia, more of Thedus, and perhaps more of Dorn's desperation to succeed. What makes Ferril a more pleasing Colorado poet to my way of thinking is his anarchic imagination, from his dialogue with a dressmaker's dummy in "Magenta" to his coyote-tour of world history in "Nocturne at Noon—1605." Here, as one small example of his work, is the lyric poem, "Morning Star":

It is tomorrow now
In this black incredible grass.

The mountains with luminous discipline
Are coming out of the blackness
To take their places one in front of the other.

I know where you are and where the river is.

You are near enough to be a far horizon.
Your body breathing is a silver edge
Of a long black mountain rising and falling slowly
Against the morning and the morning star.

Before we cannot speak again
There will be time to use the morning star
For anything, like brushing it against
A pentstemon,
Or nearly closing the lashes of our lids
As children do to make the star come down.

Or I can say to myself as if I were
A wanderer being asked where he had been
Among the hills: "There was a range of mountains
Once I loved until I could not breathe."

In this kind of lyric, borders between inner and outer states
evaporate—the subjective is the objective, and vice versa. Narrative poems, too, can open up more of the imaginal space,
more of the unparaphrasable. I wish Belle Turnbull had more
often exceeded her decorum or demolished it altogether.

Yet both of these writers were strong and original artists of
the West—important voices for anyone who wants to understand Colorado—and both are almost completely neglected
now. It is possible to live a lifetime in Colorado unaware of
Ferril's fine sonnet painted in the rotunda of the state capital.
It is possible to get a high school or college diploma in the state

without ever reading a line of its literary past. By the same token, it is possible to drive through the mountains without knowing their names or the names of the tribes and the peoples who have left their stories here. There are beautiful poetic voices in the story of Colorado, and without them we who live in the state cannot really know where we are. These lines from a Turnbull lyric, "Words About a Place," are part of the poetic struggle to name accurately where we live:

> But the words have not come up, they have not found you,
> For a town blanched at the head of a high valley,
> For what was first out of the turf returning,
> Out of the springs, out of the strong rock,
> Never the words, only the air thinned around you.

Those scars and ruins in our landscapes all have their stories, some of them in acutely fashioned lines. They ought to be heard.

A Poet of the Unaffiliated Left

THOMAS McGRATH

EARLY IN PART Two of his extraordinary long poem, *Letter to an Imaginary Friend*, Thomas McGrath described a village on the island of Skyros in Greece, and in one fluid gesture moved from that locale to his own place of origin:

Honeysuckle, lavender, oleander, osiers, olive trees, acanthus—
All leafsplit, seedshaken, buckling under the drive
Of the living orient red wind
                    constant abrasive
North Dakota
        is everywhere.
                  This town where Theseus sleeps on his hill—
Dead like Crazy Horse.
            This poverty.
                This dialectic of money—
Dakota is everywhere.
          A condition.

McGrath's vision of the human condition was rooted in his region. "Dakota is everywhere" because it contains the essential realities that define this condition in all places: mythologies and histories in symbiotic relationships, the troubled marriage of humanity and environment, the economic conditions of the status quo and one's resistance to it.

Unsympathetic readers might see only Dakota, an empty state they once drove through, where the land is flat and the winters are harsh. But that would be like looking at Manhattan and seeing only the Trump Tower. Such blinkered views miss the storied quality of place. As it happens, "Dakota" is an important landscape of the American West, or the western edge of the Middle West. It is Gatsby's birthplace; the dreams and atrocities of this region are important aspects of American culture. Thomas McGrath was one of the great poets of the West, and neglect of his work during his lifetime may have stemmed from a broad literary prejudice against western writers that no longer exists in quite the same way.

There is also the matter of his politics. A revolutionary leftist—part of what he eventually called "the unaffiliated far left"—McGrath was for some years a member of the Communist Party, and even lost an academic position in Los Angeles for refusing to cooperate with the House Un-American Activities Committee in 1953. This one brave gesture, nobly expressed in his statement to the committee, made him a hero in some circles, a pariah in others. By compromising his academic career for a number of years, eventually leaving him to teach in provincial universities in North Dakota and Minnesota, the gesture probably kept him from the networks of literary allies who would have been helpful reputation builders. Though his talent was at least equal to that of any poet of his generation, McGrath's temperament was impatient with such notions as career success. He proudly made friends with people who could do nothing to further his career because he believed in the revolutionary commune, in what the Marxist critic Christopher Caudwell had called "the collective festival, where poetry is born."

While much of American poetry became private, McGrath

spoke in a public voice. As the minimalism of William Carlos Williams took hold in poetic theory and practice, McGrath remained a poet of rhetorical flourishes, lyrical excess, puns, jokes, bawdiness, invective—a range of inventiveness and reference, of sound, fury, and hilarity, that makes most of the American poetic landscape look as flat as the Red River Valley bordering North Dakota and Minnesota.

To be sure, some critics have found a "sameness" in his work. In "The Imaginary Friendships of Tom McGrath," critic Marty Cohen wrote, "Throughout the work are scattered promising poems whose impact is lessened by an appeal to dogma, by allusions to popular styles or common measures that dip into bathos." One often wishes to edit McGrath, and his politics sometimes make it easy to disagree with him, as politics also complicate our reading of Ezra Pound. The fact that his two most supportive publishers were Alan Swallow and Sam Hamill—both important small publishers located in the West—was another symptom of his "outsider" status.

Ultimately, McGrath will be understood as a crusty individualist, neither academic nor Beat, a poet without peer who, despite his lesser work, deserves a place in the American canon. At the end of that passage in Part Two of *Letter to an Imaginary Friend*, he wrote,

> And I am only a device of memory
> To call forth into this Present the flowering dead and the living
> To enter the labyrinth and blaze the trail for the enduring journey
> Toward the round dance and commune of light . . .
>   to dive through
>   the night of rock
> (In which the statues of heroes sleep) beyond history to Origin
> To build that Legend where all journeys are one
>   where Identity
> Exists
>   where speech becomes song . . .

For McGrath the act of making the poem was tribal. Though his life was often lived in isolation, his poetry assumed a public, and it continues to find one.

A Double Voice

Thomas Matthew McGrath was born on November 20, 1916, on a farm near Sheldon, North Dakota. This is still a place of gently rolling hills, where cottonwoods line the Sheyenne River to the south, the Maple to the north, with occasional groves of box elders, shelter belts of evergreens, and a few Russian olives. It is wide open country, though not as flat as the valley of the Red River to the east, a river that flows north through Fargo and Grand Forks to Winnipeg. Associated with the sources of poetry itself, rivers were always important to McGrath.

In contrast to the predominantly Scandinavian culture of the region, McGrath's family was Irish Catholic, their life textured by the Latin rituals of itinerant priests and by the languages and folk culture of Ireland, with its resentment of empire and class. From both parents he inherited a mistrust of banks and other powerful economic interests. North Dakota was a hotbed of radical politics, and the atmosphere of McGrath's childhood was heavily politicized in terms that pitted labor, including farm labor, against the robber barons and captains of industry. When his parents married and began to farm, they were not landowners but renters. McGrath remembered his father not as a politically active man, but as one who had a basic mistrust of the rich.

Born in the year of the Easter Rebellion in Ireland, McGrath surely knew that vigorous language can be a form of revolt. (Joyce's Stephen Dedalus said that his soul fretted in the shadow of the English language, yet few have ever written English as well as Joyce.) He recalled the bookshelf in his small country school, no larger than a filing cabinet, where he found the *Iliad* and the *Odyssey* and the Norse *Edda*. A voracious reader with a powerful memory, years later he recalled his incredulity at meeting young would-be poets who had no desire to study the great literature of the past. For him, such knowledge was precious and hard-earned.

When he took his BA in 1939, McGrath won a Rhodes Scholarship to Oxford, but the advent of war forced him to postpone overseas travel. Instead he entered a master's degree program in English at Louisiana State University in Baton Rouge. As a member of the Communist Party, he distributed leaflets in black neighborhoods, and seems to have felt ambivalent about the priesthood of literary scholarship even as practiced by professors he respected, like Cleanth Brooks. At LSU McGrath met his fellow westerner Alan Swallow, who would become one of the most important independent publishers of the twentieth century. They were both students in Brooks' class on the history of criticism. Swallow had acquired a hand letterpress and was printing a book of student poems in his garage. Mc-Grath helped him out on a few occasions, and one day Swallow declared that he would like to publish McGrath's first collection. The result was a pamphlet called *First Manifesto* (1940) and it is much better than journeyman work and was favorably reviewed by the poet Selden Rodman.

After leaving a teaching position, McGrath held a number of jobs in New York: a labor organizer, a research assistant for lawyers working for leftist causes, and a welder at the Kearny Shipyards. In 1942 *The Dialectics of Love*, another small collection of his poems, was published as part of a larger book, *Three Young Poets*, edited by Alan Swallow. That year, with the permission of the Party, he entered the U. S. Army. Colorblindness kept him from flight school, and he was lucky enough not to be shipped to Europe or the South Pacific. Instead, as a member of the Army Air Force, McGrath spent two years, 1943 to 1945, in the Aleutians, most of it on the island of Amchitka. The Japanese planes had already attacked the US at Dutch Harbor to the east, and at the end of the war US troops would stage a bloody recapture of Attu to the west. But all Tom had to endure on Amchitka was the boredom of a treeless landscape, the horizontal rain, and the absurdity of military life. When he wrote, "I sit musing, ten minutes from the Jap," in a poem to his first wife called "A Letter for Marion" he was nearly being literal. The war's worst blow came in 1945 when his brother, Jimmy, was killed in a plane crash. Poems that would later deal with this event include "Blues for Jimmy" and "The World of the Perfect Tear."

After the war, Tom finally could take advantage of his Rhodes Scholarship, and spent the academic year of 1947–48 at New College, Oxford. In an interview with Frederick C. Stern he recalled, "I wrote most of *Longshot O'Leary['s Garland of Practical Poesie]* there, some of it up at Scotland during the winter Christmas vacation." These are some of McGrath's jauntiest, song-like poems, including "A Real Gone Guy," his lyric to the tune of "The Streets of Laredo":

As I walked out in the streets of Chicago,
As I stopped in a bar in Manhattan one day,
I saw a poor weedhead dressed up like a sharpie,
Dressed up like a sharpie all muggled and fey.

The essentially comic sensibilities of Auden and McGrath have been consistently misunderstood by readers who want purity in poetry—purity of diction or form or politics. Auden and McGrath were, in their different ways, too irrepressible to fit easily into the categories of others. McGrath wanted impurity, and explicitly said so many times. He also wanted breadth and variety. So it is not surprising that he was writing *Longshot O'Leary* in the same year that Swallow published his more somber first full-length book, *To Walk a Crooked Mile*.

Returning to New York after travel in Europe, he worked odd jobs and wrote pulp fiction. His marriage to Marion ended, and in 1951 he accepted a teaching position at Los Angeles State College. While he was never officially expelled from the Communist Party, he drifted away from it, and at one point co-founded his own whimsical alternative, the Ramshackle Socialist Victory Party, or R. S. V. P. He also co-founded a literary magazine, the *California Quarterly*, served on the editorial board of *Mainstream*, and wrote new poems of his own.

This relatively stable life in Southern California (including a new marriage in 1952 to Alice Greenfield) did not last long. In 1953 the House Un-American Activities Committee called McGrath before its hearings in Los Angeles. By the spring of 1954, he was out of a job and blacklisted. He worked a series of jobs after that, at the Los Angeles Stock Exchange, or laying mosaic tile, or carving wooden animals for a toymaker, or gardening. He also began to write film scripts—mostly documentary. But for the rest of the decade he had no academic position.

During the 1950s McGrath wrote *Figures from a Double World* (1955). With its arch portraits of a variety of characters, it may have carried McGrath's impersonal style as far as he could take it, and probably led to the personal recollections of *Letter*. There are important personal poems in *Figures*, especially "The World of the Perfect Tear" in memory of his brother Jimmy. But much of the book reads something like the "Robinson" poems of Weldon Kees, though McGrath's anger is less autobiographical, more allegorical, turned outward at the mendacity of American life. Though some of McGrath's poems now appear merely dogmatic—like leftist alternatives to Yeats's fascist marching songs—in his best work his love of the word, the delightful intoxication of poetry itself, saves him from mere propaganda. In aesthetics as well as politics, he was unaffiliated and difficult to pin down. The most powerful poem in *Figures from the Double World* is his "Ode for the American Dead in Asia," a sequence of three sonnets memorializing the Korean War. "God love you now," it memorably begins, "if no one else will ever, / Corpse in the paddy, or dead on a high hill / In the fine and ruinous summer of a war / You never wanted." It is significant that this Marxist poet could liberate himself sufficiently from materialism to evoke God with simultaneous ritual and irony. When poetry takes on a ritual voice, its elevation makes us aware that such language is not at the level of our daily muddle. McGrath could write with the ritual voice because he held a double view of poetry itself. It served purposes, and it was itself a purpose, a way of being in the world.

Letter to an Imaginary Friend

"The poem began one afternoon in 1954 at the house of the poet Don Gordon, in Los Angeles." So begins an elucidation of *Letter* in "McGrath on McGrath" (*Dream Champ*, 1982). After praising such "Lost Poets" as Gordon and Naomi Replansky, he refers to his own trepidation at writing a long poem. "I suppose Don knew instantly that it was more lack of nerve than anything else that was stopping me. He gave me the obvious advice: Begin and see what happens." McGrath went home and made his start. Line one of the poem is in quotes as if overheard from conversation: "From here it is necessary to ship all bodies east." It's the end of Manifest Destiny, or as Louis Simpson would later put it in his ironic take on Whitman, "the end of the Open Road." The mysterious ruefulness of McGrath's opening alludes to American myths gone wrong. He records the process of writing as he writes himself back in time, "On a mission of armed revolutionary memory!" It will not be merely a nostalgic backward look, for, as he writes later, "Nostalgia is decayed dynamite." It will be the long poem that attempts to contain the whole man. Amy Clampitt, writing in the *Nation* (November 6, 1989), would later call his long poem "by turns fierce, somber, rollicking, and outrageous—a simmering *olla podrida* of an epic, from which there is the urge at moments, perhaps, to turn away. Only one doesn't, much as one can't tear oneself away from a party that is getting out of hand."

Letter to an Imaginary Friend evolved over more than thirty years, from the blacklisted fifties to McGrath's teaching years in North Dakota and Minnesota. Part One was published by Swallow in 1962, Parts One and Two together in 1970. Parts Three and Four would be published by Copper Canyon Press in 1985. In the intervening years Alan Swallow would die of a heart attack in Denver. McGrath would be married for a third time, to the Greek-American Eugenia Johnson, who in 1969 would bear him a son, often called Tomasito in the poems. McGrath would even kill a man and briefly go to jail for it. There would be other changes and developments, some of which were recorded in the completed poem, and by the time its final sections were published McGrath's own health would be severely compromised.

Any thorough discussion of a poem as big, significant, and unruly as *Letter* would require volumes, but in this short space we can at least touch upon its themes and high points. McGrath himself would discuss its shape in terms of spirals, like the diagram of DNA he prints in Part Four, and its technique by comparison to cuts in a film (he was an experienced, professional writer of scripts). In "McGrath on McGrath" he makes it clear that he had given a great deal of thought to the problem of the long poem: "Poe was 100% wrong. It is the *'short'* poem which is a contradiction in terms. In reality there are only *long* poems and the void. It is true that what we appear to get are 'aphorisms, epigrams, songs, song-like poems' and so on. But these are only fragments of the long poem which the poet somehow failed to write, that long poem which he will go on trying to write by fits and starts his whole life long." This is the theory by which the collected poems of Yeats, for example, can be read the way we read *Leaves of Grass*—as one lifelong project in multiple versions. McGrath considers long poems by Crane, Homer, MacLeish, Pound, Williams, and Ginsberg, all of which he finds unhelpful as models. Dante, too, would be a source for images in *Letter*, as well as Wordsworth and Blake. But McGrath's long poem is ultimately *sui generis*. By turns narrative and fragmentary, lyrical and prosaic, historical, mythical, autobiographical, surrealistic, and visionary, riddled with puns, allusions, neologisms, high and low humor, revolutionary but in some of its attitudes "politically incorrect," it is the kind of wild creation that invites comparison to great writers of the past.

Parts One and Two contain the most realistic and accessible sections, though one could say the same of some of the Christmas section in Part Three. Generally, the shorter final sections are wilder, more difficult, at times even trying the patience of sympathetic readers. The central metaphor of Part One is Eden, the Fall from Grace spelled out in the young McGrath's dawning awareness of political struggle. Significantly, the crucial scene is a communal one, a harvest time in North Dakota sometime in the mid-1920s. These were the last years of the steam threshers, some of which can still be found rusting in farm communities like Rollag, Minnesota. The vision of ideal community carries with it the image of a technology predating Marx:

Feathered in steam like a great tormented beast
The engine roared and laughed, dreamed and complained,
And the petcocks dripped and sizzled; and under its fiery gut
Stalactites formed from the handhold's rheumy slobbers.
—Mane of sparks, metallic spike of its voice,
The mile-long bacony crackle of burning grease!
There the engineer sat, on the high drivers,
Aloof as a God. Filthy. A hunk of waste
Clutched in one gauntleted hand, in the other the oilcan
Beaked and long-necked as some exotic bird;
Wreathed in smoke, in the clatter of loose eccentrics.
And the water-monkey, back from the green quiet of the river
With a full tank, was rolling a brown quirly,
(A high school boy) hunkered in the dripping shade
Of the water tender, in the tall talk and acrid sweat
Of the circle of spitting stiffs whose cloud-topped bundle-racks

Waited their turns at the feeder.
And the fireman: goggled, shirtless, a flashing three-tined fork,
Its handle charred, stuck through the shiny metallic
Lip of the engine, into the flame, smoky
Firebox of its heart.
Myself: straw-monkey. Jester at court.

In what is surely one of the great descriptive passages in American poetry, McGrath mythologizes the machine and the workers, makes them figures from a primordial world. And the whole long description funnels down to the small boy called out to work because one of the men was missing. "Was it hard?" he asks later. "No. Everyone wanted to help me." This is what McGrath means by the commune, the community united in work.

The gesture of writing a letter to an imaginary friend seems child-like in its simplicity, evoking the despair of so many poets who wonder what became of their audience. In interviews, however, McGrath was fond of echoing Emerson, saying that each of us lives two lives: once as a private self, then as a Representative Man. His method in *Letter* is to begin with autobiography and move toward allegory. The boy working as straw-monkey out in the fields is the man writing the poem, who recalls, "My father took me as far as he could that summer, / Those midnights, mostly, back from his long haul." There was another man, McGrath informs us, who could take the boy further: "But mostly Cal, one of the bundle teamsters, / My sun-blackened Virgil of the spitting circle, / Led me from depth to depth." The literary self-consciousness of the allusion to Virgil brings with it images of journey, harrowing hell, and tribal identity. Even the six-beat line, the basic line for many of his strongest passages, is a borrowing from Homer. (Later poets like Seamus Heaney and Derek Walcott, both Nobel Prize-winners, would use such allusive structures for their longer poems. McGrath deserves at least to be in their company.)

But if Cal is his Virgil, it is only for a time. Cal is a Wobbly: "He read *The Industrial Worker,* / Though I didn't know what the paper was at the time. / The last of the real Wobs— . . . ." Cal teaches him to shoot and to handle horses. "He wanted me to grow without growing too fast for myself. / A good teacher, a brother."

In a crucial scene, Cal gets into a fight over labor issues with one of McGrath's uncles and is severely beaten. The scene has an almost Biblical force:

> Cal spoke for the men and my uncle cursed him.
> I remember that ugly sound, like some animal cry touching me
> Deep and cold, and I ran toward them
> And the fighting started.
> My uncle punched him. I heard the breaking crunch
> Of his teeth going and the blood leaped out of his mouth
> Over his neck and shirt—I heard their gruntings and strainings
> Like love at night or men working hard together,
> And heard the meaty thumpings, like beating a grain sack
> As my uncle punched his body—I remember the dust
> Jumped from his shirt.

In the wake of this violence, which seems to upset everyone in McGrath's family, the boy runs off alone to the river. There, among the trees, "Runeless I stood in the green rain / Of the leaves." Away from people, he seeks a kind of solace— these lines might be compared to Whitman's "Out of the Cradle Endlessly Rocking." The scene ends when he is back with his family, hears from his mother that Cal won't eat, and from his father: "Hard times, Old Timer."

> I sat in the lantern's circle, the world of men,
> And heard Cal breathe in his stall.
>
> > An army of crickets
> Rasped in my ear.
>
> > "Don't hate anybody,"

My father said.

I went toward the house through the dark.

When Chapter III of Part One ends, the community has been broken.

Chapter IV is McGrath's paean to budding sexuality: "O great kingdom of Fuck! And myself: plenipotentiary!" These passages evoke adolescence's hyperbolic obsessions, while Chapter V begins, "Love and hunger!—that is my whole story." But the hunger here is for learning and self-improvement. The Depression was on when he went away to college—first to Moorhead:

> And the first man I met was some kind of dean.
> O excellent title!
> What did it mean? Did the tumbleweed
> Blowing out of Saskatchewan know it?
> A man, anyhow, thin as a rail and mean
> As a cross-barred barbwire gate, with a flat face to him
> Like Picasso's Vallauris plates; all piss and moment,
> A pithy, pursy bastard, like a quidnunc espaliered
> Against the ass of the North Wind.
> He sat there like a chilly Lutheran Buddha,
> All two dimensions of him— . . . .

The poem has moved far from lyrical remembrance, deep into invective and satire. Like Auden, he shows a fondness for mixing high and low diction—the Latin of *quidnunc* set "Against the ass of the North Wind"—but McGrath's macaronic language has a fully American flavor to it, a gruffness akin to Pound's. He delights in sending readers to the dictionary, and the breadth and depth of his word-hoard is part of his poem's carnival spirit.

His education interrupted by "hard times," he returns home, where in Chapter VII he gives us a Frostian woodcutting scene:

> And did we burn?
> We burned with a cold flame.

And did we freeze?
We froze in bunches of five.
And did we complain?
We did, we did, we did.

Chapters VIII through XI are fairly straight autobiography, vividly written, the *Bildungsroman* of "Tom Fool," still a jester. We follow his Marxist education, his university years in Grand Forks and Baton Rouge, his meetings with Marion Points, Alan Swallow, and Cleanth Brooks, then the war and the Aleutians. Part One of *Letter* ends in Chapter XII at the level of song or chant. These are McGrath's pagan beatitudes:

> Blesséd be the blood hung like a bell in my body's branching tree;
> Blesséd be dung and honey;
> Blesséd be the strong key of my sex in her womb, by cock and by cunt blesséd
> The electric bird of desire, dropped in the locked-room mysteries of country charm;
> Blesséd be my writing hand and arm and the black lands of my secret heart.

The passage goes on for three large-format pages, a strong rhythmic conclusion signed *"Los Angeles, 1955."* It was the year before Ginsberg's *Howl and Other Poems*, but McGrath had begun, on his own and with far less fanfare, what Jack Beeching would later call "his quiet lifelong counterattack" against the dominant culture.

Part Two begins where Part One left off, with song, but finds McGrath in Greece, thinking "Dakota is everywhere." Rather than forwarding the plot in strict chronological fashion, McGrath circles back over Part One in an "eccentric spiral." The "present" of the opening—his life in Greece with Eugenia in the 1960s—will contain the past the way a tree's rings are its former skins inside its present one. The poem will also reflect all of the places in which it was written—Part Two is signed, "*North Dakota—Skyros—Ibiza—Agaete—Guadalajara, 1968.*" He recalls the poem's genesis with the liberating advice of Don Gordon. He recalls his work as a labor organizer in New York. And he recalls the feeling of waiting for the Revolution, the great change to come upon the world.

It is also in Part Two that McGrath introduces his next major symbol:

> Wait for the Angel.
> SAQUASOHUH:
> the blue star
> Far off, but coming.
> Invisible yet.
> Announcing the Fifth
> World
> (Hopi prophecy)
> world we shall enter soon:
> When the Blue Star Kachina, its manifested spirit,
> Shall dance the *kisonvi* for the first time.

The appropriation of Native American mythology may put some readers off, but they should know that it is not done in the spirit of Liberal sentimentality. In 1960 he had married Eugenia, and the same year they founded the journal *Crazy Horse*, announcing later in a manifesto, "We the Irregulars of Crazy Horse, Ghost Dancers of the essential existential Solidarity, now summon into being the hosts of the new resistance. Give up those bird-cages built for lions! Alienation is not enough! Jawsmiths, nightwalkers, moonbirds: Unite!" Whimsical, dismissive of academic formalism, and well beyond mere politics, the manifesto compares McGrath's own resistance to that of the eradicated Ghost Dancers his father had heard about at Fort Ransom. By the time he wrote Part Two of *Letter*, America had not yet seen the movies that would equate the Indian Wars and Vietnam in the popular imagination, such as *Soldier Blue* and *Little Big Man*, and certainly nothing like the later sentimentality of *Dances with Wolves*. Readers now might assume that McGrath was a "wannabe," a white man yearning to be Indian. But he wasn't. He was a Westerner; he grew up with Indians in close proximity, and he could not escape the fact that their story was part of his own. It was one of the deep national wounds of America.

McGrath's use of Hopi ceremony and story, no less legitimate than Eliot's use of *The Golden Bough*, is based upon Frank Waters's *Book of the Hopi* (1963), which demonstrates the universality of narrative sources. According to Waters, Hopi narratives describe at first a progress through three worlds. "The Fourth World, the present one, is the full expression of man's ruthless materialism and imperialistic will; and man himself reflects the overriding gross appetites of the flesh." But the Fifth World will come "when a *kachina* [an embodied spirit] removes his mask during a dance in the plaza before uninitiated children. For a while there will be no more ceremonies, no more faith. Then Oraibi [the Rock on High] will be rejuvenated with its faith and ceremonies, marking the start of a new cycle of Hopi life." The blue star *kachina*, Saquasohuh, is not the Angel of Class Struggle barring the gate to Eden with a flaming sword, but the Angel of a new Annunciation.

In the definitive edition of the complete *Letter*, published in 1997 by Copper Canyon Press, Parts One and Two take up 271 pages, Parts Three and Four just over 130. Completed in 1984, the whole poem does have a feeling of rushing to its conclusion. Now living in Moorhead, teaching at Moorhead State University and the father of a young son, McGrath harkened back to his Catholic childhood for an image of community. The star of Jesus and the blue star of Saquasohuh are both important symbols in *Letter*. But, as if to be certain that we understand it is not the institution of the Church he extols, McGrath gives us in Part Three a magnificently Joycean confession scene. In its vocabulary alone, it is one of the most outrageous and inventive passages in the entire poem.

"I am guilty of chrestomathy, Father."

He lets out a grunt in Gaelic,
Shifting out of the Latin to get a fresh purchase on sin.
"And?"
"Barratry, Father.
"And minerology . . .
"Agatism and summer elements . . .
"Skepticism about tooth fairies . . .
"Catachresis and pseudogogy . . ."

From the unity of family at Christmas to the absurdity of this confession, McGrath moves to the camaraderie of poets, mostly male, living and dead, listing his father the storyteller among them. Then he circles back to the family "gathered now by the river of Latin in our little church." As Part One ended with song, or chanted beatitudes, Part Three ends with an oratorio in musical parts, dissolving finally in fragmentation that echoes *The Waste Land*. Part Four makes a great heave toward conclusion, beginning with the line "NOW MOVE ALL SYMBOLS THREE LEAPS TO THE LEFT!" From there it flows on through a speedy lyrical deconstruction of family history, the spirals of DNA, etc. These fragments, though, are not shored against anyone's ruins; they are rushed through, headlong, as McGrath recaps the Hopi journey through the Four Worlds toward the Fifth, the blue star *kachina*. Perhaps he has thrown coherence to the winds in these final pages. Perhaps he is like Dante coming finally up to the shimmering limits of the word.

Echoes and Passages

When Jack Beeching went to Fargo in the late 1960s, he witnessed Tom's alienation from academic life. He tells of a party where they met a psychologist just back from aiding the war effort in Vietnam, having experimented with such techniques as dropping broken glass into rice paddies to break Vietnamese morale.

> In a deceptively quiet voice McGrath, who in his day had seen the wartime Aleutians, the jimcrow South and the New York dock strike, asked him, "Just what did you think you were doing?"
>
> "Fighting Communism."
>
> "Then come outside and fight me."

McGrath was unusual in the consistency of his convictions. In 1974 he met Sam Hamill, who would become his friend and, at Copper Canyon, the primary publisher of his poetry. It was typical of McGrath that such matters as writing and publishing were related more to friendship than to commerce and career.

Despite the relative stability of his job, his personal life was troubled. In the summer of 1975, at a time when he and Eugenia were living separately and often arguing about Tomasito, McGrath killed a man. He wrote to Sam Hamill about the event roughly two weeks after it occurred:

> [He] was breaking into my wife's house where she and my little son were at. He was crazy drunk, with a history of this kind of violence and it was his intention to kill my wife—maybe all of us. Or to get himself killed. He had been warned off by police during the day, by my wife in the evening when he called, very drunk, and by myself as he tried to break down first the back and then the front door. I fired a warning shot and then as the door was caving in—I thought he had an ax—I fired at random thru the door.

The letter soon takes a strange turn, especially when we consider McGrath's longstanding sympathies for Native Americans:

What makes it hard: he was an Indian + the white law is ter-rified of the power of the nearby reservation. . . . So: instead of a coroner's inquiry + a verdict of justifiable homicide I was charged with 3rd degree murder and manslaughter, jailed + am now out on $10,000 bail.

By the time he wrote the letter, Tom had begun to rationalize events. With no trace of concern for the dead man, he turns immediately to his own legal and financial problems, declaring that he is "in a scapegoat situation."

Jack Beeching was in New York when he learned of the shooting, and immediately flew to Minnesota to help his friend. His memoir gives sketchy details of the shooting, more about the subsequent grand jury trial, which he witnessed him-self. He describes the difficulty Tom's family and friends had in getting him to prepare himself to appear before a jury, to dress properly and watch his words. He also describes in detail the defense put on by McGrath's attorney, climaxing in a moment of drama when "the actual shot-perforated door" was carried into court "to prove Tom had fired blind. . . ." In the end, the charges were dropped. But these events certainly clouded Mc-Grath's life, while his marriage to Eugenia remained troubled by drinking and continued fighting over their son.

McGrath's health was also breaking down. A letter of Oc-tober 10, 1980, reports a "semi-diabetic condition" necessitat-ing a change of diet. It also details some work done toward a new book of poems, eventually titled *Passages Toward the Dark* (1982)—McGrath ruefully jokes about getting the Pulitzer for it, knowing it will not happen. And he mentions work on a film script—one of fourteen he would write, including his un-filmed adaptation of Frederick Manfred's novel, *Conquering Horse*, for director Michael Cimino (who had quoted McGrath in his film *Thunderbolt and Lightfoot*). The letters to Hamill in the early 1980s record feelings of depression, isolation, the bur-den of work, and more fights over custody of Tomasito. In 1979 a car accident gave him whiplash, and over time the pain in his neck and shoulder became unbearable. He underwent surgery to correct the condition, but the operation went terribly wrong. "I'm now about 60% paralyzed + in worse pain, wheel chair etc.," he wrote in August 1983. It was the beginning of a run of bad luck. While he would regain some mobility, one leg dragged and he often used a cane. His circulation was so poor in his left hand that he often wore a heavy glove to keep it warm. For the last six years of his life he referred to himself as a cripple, suffering chronic pain that increased his sense of isolation.

Still, he was publishing poems and gaining recognition. He moved to the Twin Cities to be close both to Tomasito and to more of Minnesota's cultural life, and was living alone in an apartment near the Loft, an arts organization that was beginning to recognize his work. Once he had been championed mostly by leftist magazines and small journals like California's *kayak*, a feisty periodical edited by George Hitchcock, who had himself performed with comic aplomb before the House Un-American Activities Committee. Now McGrath's work appeared regularly in *The American Poetry Review* and other prominent journals. He had already won an Amy Lowell Travelling Poetry Fellowship, followed by a Guggenheim, various arts board fellowships, and an award from the Academy of American Poets that allowed him to travel to Nicaragua. His new books, *Passages Toward the Dark* and *Echoes Inside the Labyrinth* (the latter published by Thunder's Mouth Press in 1983), both contained important McGrath poems mixed in with lesser work. *Selected Poems 1938–1988*, edited and introduced by Sam Hamill, was published by Copper Canyon, and won both the Shelley Memorial Award and the Lenore Marshall/*Nation* Award.

Gratified by his growing reputation, he complained that his health had deteriorated to the point where he could no longer write without assistance. In and out of hospitals, he began to compile a final collection, *Death Song*, which appeared post-humously in 1991. The book contains a mixture of mid-length poems and the shorter ones he composed when he could no longer comfortably hold a pen, including his "Song of the Open Road" dedicated to Reginald Gibbons: "Protected from all running dogs / Through Hell and through Gone I go: / Guided by the great Saint Yes / And his master: great Saint No."

After his death, there were memorials for McGrath in Chicago and Minneapolis, as well as the college towns on the Red River of the North. His colleagues at Moorhead State University planted a cottonwood in the quad with a small plaque containing one of McGrath's most touching short poems:

You out there, so secret.
What makes you think you're alone

The survival of any true talent through life's trials always carries an air of the miraculous. Thomas McGrath's weaker poems, marred by self-righteousness and sentimentality, will fall away, leaving a core of brilliant, idiosyncratic work, especially in his long poem of the unaffiliated left. Calling him a regional writer does not quite hit the mark any more than calling him a political poet does. His maker's mark was a record of struggle, the effort at human liberation we never quite achieve.

The Western Prophets

WALLACE STEGNER
AND EDWARD ABBEY

Last year a Colorado rancher showed me a photograph he had taken from a small plane. It was of a dust cloud, thousands of feet high and many miles wide, rolling over the state's eastern prairies toward the Front Range of the Rocky Mountains. "It's like the Thirties," he said. "We haven't learned a thing." While we have outgrown the disastrous adage "Rain follows the plow" that helped bring on the Dust Bowl, we pay too little heed to unplanned population growth and water shortages in the West. Droughts, floods, and fires are naturally recurring events in this fragile and friable region—anyone who lives here must contend with them in one way or another.

In *All the Wild That Remains*, David Gessner probes the myths and arguments that have made the American West the inspiring and dangerous place it is through the lives of two of the region's major writers, Wallace Stegner and Edward Abbey. Mr. Gessner, an environmentalist and founder of the magazine *Ecotone*, describes his book as "a hybrid animal—part dueling biography, part travel narrative, part meditation, part criticism, part nature writing." His endeavor to understand two strong literary personalities is itself a quest for the good life— a quest to find joy in nature and to understand the limits of individual liberty.

Abbey (1927–89) briefly studied writing with Stegner (1909–93) at Stanford in the 1950s, and the men warily followed each other's careers. Stegner had compensated for a tumultuous childhood with civility and reserve. His father, a violent dreamer, moved the family constantly, from Saskatchewan to Seattle to Utah, eventually killing a woman and then "shooting himself in a shabby hotel room in downtown Salt Lake City." Though Stegner avowed the West as "hope's native home," he also despaired over its transience and lack of community.

Born in hillbilly Pennsylvania, Edward Abbey fell in love with the West at 18, seeing in the desert rocks, canyons, and rivers a space for both reverence and anarchy. He was a hard-drinking wild man—married five times—and "the least pious of environmentalists," fond of guns and tossing his beer cans by the side of the road. As Gessner puts it, Abbey was "lecherous, combative, unpredictable, contradictory." Yet "all who knew him said he was actually quiet and reserved in person. Not on the page, where he could sometimes be as subtle as a whoopee cushion." For many, he will always be the author of *The Monkey Wrench Gang* (1975), an unruly novel about anarchists plotting to blow up the Glen Canyon Dam on the Colorado River. Mr. Gessner explains that monkey wrenching is usually small-time eco-sabotage: "fighting the despoiling of the West by cutting down billboards and pulling up surveyors' stakes and pouring sugar into the gas tanks of bulldozers." It made him a cult figure, and Mr. Gessner strives to find the real man and the real writer under the layers of legend and controversy.

By contrast, "Stegner spent a lifetime ripping aside the veils of western myths and rationalizations," Mr. Gessner notes.

The proud cowboy can as easily be a nut with a gun as an iconic loner. Stegner called his own temperament "quiet, recessive, skeptical, and watchful," but he was also a man of strong opinions, fuming in an essay, "no one who has ever studied western history can cling to the belief that the Nazis invented genocide." He was a literary giant—Abbey thought him worthy of the Nobel Prize. As a biographer he helped shape the canon of Western literature, writing on John Wesley Powell, the far-seeing explorer of the Colorado River, and Bernard DeVoto, the popular historian of the West. In his short stories and novels like *The Spectator Bird* (1977) and *Crossing to Safety* (1987) readers will find both restraint and psychological penetration. Western landscapes are particularly important in *The Big Rock Candy Mountain* (1943), an epic of foiled aspiration, and the Pulitzer Prize-winning *Angle of Repose* (1971), based partly on the letters of Mary Hallock Foote about her travels in the "Old West."

One can also turn to essay collections like *The Sound of Mountain Water* (1969) and *Where the Bluebird Sings to the Lemonade Springs* (1992) for some of his most visionary writing about the region. The first of these includes his famous "Wilderness Letter," one of the foundational documents of contemporary environmentalism. Stegner was addressing the Outdoor Recreation Resources Review Commission, which Congress had created in 1958 to assess the state of America's wilds. His words helped politicians and activists frame the 1964 Wilderness Act and give a westerner's perspective on the national soul: "Something will have gone out of us as a people if we ever let the remaining wilderness be destroyed; . . . if we pollute the last clear air and dirty the last clean streams and push our paved roads through the last of the silence."

Gessner is an Easterner who attended university in Colorado, and in what he calls "an essential American trope," felt himself remade by the "freedom" of the West. In his book, he returns several times to the region, alone or with his good-humored daughter, in order to investigate not only the lives of his two protagonists, but also the effects of growth, global warming, and the fracking boom on landscapes he loves. His personal pilgrimage alternates with mini-biographies of his two main subjects, interviews with people who knew them, and reportage. He also makes clear distinctions between the American West as it is—the geology, wildlife, and weather, its cities and crowded recreational spaces—and the American West as it is *written*. His own literary aspirations have been shaped not just by Stegner and Abbey but by others like Wendell Berry and Terry Tempest Williams.

"Transcendence," Abbey wrote in his journal. "It is this which haunts me night and day. The desire to transcend my own limits, to exceed myself, to become more than I am. Why? I don't know. To transcend this job, this work, this place, this kind of life—for the sake of something superlative, supreme, exalting." A connection with the sublime otherness of mountains and canyons runs through most of what he wrote. He wanted to "write like the desert": "Hard distinctions, precise outlines—but each thing, suggesting, somehow, everything else. As in truth each thing does." While there are fine portions in novels like *Black Sun* (1971) and *The Fool's Progress* (1988), Abbey did his best writing in nonfiction, sometimes betraying his academic training as a philosopher. His masterpiece, *Desert Solitaire* (1968), soulfully unpacks his seasons as a park ranger in Utah, where his semi-fictional persona is "a man living in nature, a man passing his days watching cloud formations" over monuments of rock.

Where Abbey flouted authority—and inspired anarchist groups like Earth First!—Stegner worked more quietly. He helped foster the national campaign in the early 1950s that stopped the Echo Park Dam on the Green River and created the Dinosaur National Monument in Colorado and Utah. He was long active in the Sierra Club, advocating a deeper awareness of the West's aridity and the importance of its rivers. As

Gessner notes, "To call the Colorado River the lifeblood of the West is no exaggeration." Its drought-diminished flow has now reached crisis stage, because "whole cities and mini societies have grown up around their negotiated share of this particular river." Mr. Gessner has stern words about water use in Phoenix, "the electric hive of Vegas, and the greatest water slurpers of them all, the residents of California." Stegner was slow to see the destructive effects of the dams on the Colorado. It was Abbey who wrote, "There is no lack of water here, unless you try to establish a city where no city should be." Eventually, his anarchist rage inspired resistance that sometimes went to extremes, such as the 1998 eco-terrorist arson at Vail ski resort by members of the Earth Liberation Front.

The contradictions abound. Terry Tempest Williams suggests to Gessner that Abbey was the real conservative, "Wally, forever the radical." Many of Abbey's anti-government attitudes seem aligned with today's Tea Partiers, while Stegner's communal values reflect a mainstream liberalism. One virtue of Mr. Gessner's book is that he never reduces either man to simplistic categories, but sees in both personalities possible life models, men who loved nature and felt keenly the limits on human liberty.

Abbey died at sixty-two of esophageal bleeding and was buried, illegally, in the desert. The story is wonderful—only adding to the burgeoning myth. Friends, some of whom figure as characters in his books, broke him out of the hospital and took him into the desert to die. Eventually they moved him to his writing shack near Tucson, and when he finally stopped breathing they forged a death certificate and escaped with his corpse into the wilderness. Mr. Gessner considered going in search of the grave: "I knew I would likely be able to find the spot: I had good contacts, old friends of Ed's, and thought it wouldn't be too hard to figure out the location. But when I got to the Abbey library in Tucson I changed my mind. The plan had the whiff of grave-robbing to it."

Not everyone has been so cautious. Mr. Gessner's book arrives at the same time as a smaller one by Sean Prentiss, an academic and outdoor enthusiast. *Finding Abbey* is subtitled "The Search for Edward Abbey and His Hidden Desert Grave," and one's heart sinks at the prospect of sensationalism. Like Mr. Gessner, Mr. Prentiss is an Easterner who came West to attend college—in this case Western State College in Gunnison, Colorado. But Mr. Prentiss's love affair with the landscape has been a devoted one. He knows the challenging summits of peaks like Mount Blanca in the Sangre de Cristo Range, and he has built himself a cabin near the Continental Divide.

Yet the book is much too credulous:

> The four of us will sit to eat while Hector the dog lies at my feet. The ghost of Abbey will reside in the room. I will hear him whisper from the loft, his words ringing from *The Fool's Progress*, "This world, these friends, what more could a body want?" *Yes, Abbey, yes.* That's why I drove hard and fast these last two days.

Prentiss frets too much, comparing himself to his heroes and revealing a youthful narcissism in the solitary Western romance. Like Gessner, he locates and interviews Abbey's inner circle of friends, and in these faithfully recorded scenes his book finally catches fire—including a conversation with Doug Peacock, the ex-Green Beret and model for Abbey's monkey-wrenching Hayduke, who in real life keeps a .357 Magnum by his side. The final chapters of Mr. Prentiss's quest are suspenseful and winning, and despite its weaker moments, *Finding Abbey* is a touching book.

The idea of the American West—of the individual set free in wide open spaces with few rules and little government interference—has inspired millions to migrate here. But these are shallow roots and create a dangerous nostalgia. The region's best writers remind us who we are by connecting us to the land and its often troubling stories. Both Gessner and Prentiss went west as naïve romantics, but their journeys taught them to see the elemental beauty, the dryness and violence as distinct realities. We still need the "spiritual resource" of the wild, Gessner writes, but "With each generation we settle for less wilderness, less freedom, less space." As different as they were, Abbey and Stegner became prophets of an endangered place. "The boosters have been there from the beginning," Stegner wrote, "to oversell the West as the Garden of the World, the flowing well of opportunity, the stamping ground of the self-reliant." The greatest virtue of these new books will be to return us to such vision.

2015

Acknowledgments

SOME OF THE ESSAYS in this book have been previously published in different form:

"Letter from Tasmania," "Travelers," "The Unseeable, Unsayable World," "Reading Greece," "Man of Action, Man of Letters," "Awe for Auden," and "Ariel and Co." (Les Murray section) in the *Hudson Review*; "Creating a Literary Hero" and "Voices, Places" in the *Sewanee Review*; "Belle Turnbull's Western Narrative" in *Belle Turnbull: On the Life and Work of an American Master*; "A Poet of the Unaffiliated Left" in *Scribner's American Writers*, vol. X, ed. Jay Parini; "Ariel and Co." (Cally Conan-Davies section) in *Voltage Poetry*; "The Silk Road of Poetry," "Walking to the Heart of Greece," "So He'll Go No More A-Roving," "The News from Everywhere," "A Mad Master of Modernism," "The Western Prophets," and "To Humanize the 'Inhumanist'" in the *Wall Street Journal*.

The author and publisher gratefully acknowledge the following additional sources:

Thomas Hornsby Ferril, "Morning Song," from *Thomas Hornsby Ferril and the American West* (Fulcrum Publishing, 1996). Used by permission.

Kevin Hart, *Wild Track: New and Selected Poems* (University of Notre Dame Press, 2015). Used by permission. Quotations from *The Dark Gaze: Maurice Blanchot and the Sacred* (University of Chicago Press, 2004). Used by permission.

Thomas McGrath, *Selected Poems: 1938–1988* (Copper Canyon Press, 1988); *Letter to an Imaginary Friend: Parts I–IV* (Copper Canyon Press, 1997); and *Death Song* (Copper Canyon Press, 1991). Used by permission.

David J. Rothman and Jeffrey R. Villines, editors, *Belle Turnbull: On the Life and Work of an American Master* (Pleiades Press, 2017). Used by permission.